Dante and Beatrice gaze upon Empyrean. Scene from Dante's 'Divine Comedy', illustrated by Gustave Dore.

CW01464518

The
Near - Death
Experience

(A REVIEW OF THE LITERATURE)

by Tony Meyer, Ph.D.

To Diane.

Contents

		Page
Objectives	....	4
Foreword	....	5
Introduction	....	8
Chapter 1	**The classic near-death experience**	10
Chapter 2	**Component features of the near-death experience**	15
	1. The out-of-body experience (OBE).	15
	2. The tunnel, the light and the world beyond.	26
	3. The meeting with others.	37
	4. Reviewing life events.	46
	5. Visions of terror.	50
Chapter 3	**NDEs in the pre-adolescent population.**	55
Chapter 4	**Some 'special' near-death experiences.**	62
	1. Total brain shutdown.	62
	2. NDEs experienced by the congenitally blind.	68
Chapter 5	**The Afterglow.**	74

Chapter 6 **Some Celebrity NDEs** 77

Chapter 7 **The Shared-death experience.** 84

Chapter 8 **Cultural aspects to NDEs.** 90

      1. Hinduism.   90

      2. Islam.   94

      3. Buddhism.   96

Chapter 9 **Psychometric scales to measure NDEs.** 103

Chapter 10 **The 'AWARE' research study.** 110

Chapter 11 **Looking for explanations.** 115

      1. Neurophysiological changes following cardiac arrest 115

      2. Recreational drugs.   117

      3. Blood gases.   118

      4. The depersonalisation model.   120

      5. The dying brain hypothesis.   122

      6. Birth memories.   123

Chapter 12 **NDEs and the nature of consciousness** 125

Appendix **A Profile of Leading Research Workers in the Field of Near-Death Studies.**...........................129

Bibliography 133

<u>*Objectives*</u>

The intention in writing this book was simply to give the reader a brief overview of the ever-burgeoning collection of literature concerning what has become known as The Near-Death-Experience (NDE).

In no way do I pretend to present startling new evidence for life in the hereafter. Rather, I have attempted to bring together the personal recollections of people who, though deeply unconscious and at the point of death, were able to recount clear and lucid memories of their resuscitation and other events when full consciousness had returned.

Commonly reported and sequential episodes in the NDE are examined, together with methods designed to quantify the phenomenon.

The influence of cultural background is discussed and ongoing research projects are outlined.

Finally, explanations are sought from the diverse fields of philosophy, theology, biochemistry, physiology, psychology, psychiatry and even quantum physics.

My aim has been to present this concise review in readable form, not for cutting edge scientists in the field, but for those who are unaware of the NDE phenomenon or those with some knowledge who wish to learn more.

The bibliography section provides many references for more in depth insights.

Foreword

It was March 1961 and my 9th birthday was just a few weeks away. My great-grandmother's health had been failing for many months and the doctor was a frequent presence at her bedside. My parents drove the ten miles from Exeter to the small Devonshire market town of Ottery St. Mary for the regular Sunday afternoon visit and I was taken with them. On returning from school one day, I was told we were all going over to see 'Great-Gran' once again. My first thought was one of frustration and I can remember distinctly blurting out, 'Oh, not again!'. I was then told quietly and succinctly that this would probably be the last time I would be able to see her. I felt acutely guilty about my outburst and fell silent. Hardly a word was spoken in the car on the way to her house.

There were three people in her dimly-lit bedroom when we arrived, the doctor and my mother's parents. Edith lay motionless, as if in deep sleep and I thought she had already died. There were whispered exchanges between those assembled, none of which were designed for my hearing. A chair was brought in for me to sit on and I gathered the end was near. Mixed emotions swirled in my head. I wanted to rush out of the room and cry, yet I was somehow fascinated by the whole process and wanted to be included. Soft words were spoken to the old lady, none of which elicited a response and I felt the situation had become faintly embarrassing as nobody seemed to know quite what to do.

Then it happened. Edith opened her eyes and struggled to sit up, which she managed to do without help. I hadn't seen her in this position for a very long time and I assumed, that by some miracle, she had made a recovery and that the recent words spoken to her were not in vain. There she was, her ashen face suddenly vibrant and smiling, looking straight ahead, yet she seemed oblivious to all of us around her, for she gazed towards a wall at the end of the bed where no one was standing. Stretching out her arms, she uttered one clear word, 'George' and seemed to nod her head. She was then helped to lie back down and she resumed her slumbers.

I was sure she would live on, but within the hour her breathing had stopped and she had passed away. The conversation in the car on the way home was muted and restrained, but I later learned that George was her husband who had died in 1937 and I was told that my great-grandmother had experienced a 'death-bed vision'. I wanted to ask more but there was an air of reluctance in the family to discuss the matter further, though I felt everyone had been profoundly affected by what they had witnessed.

It wasn't until 1977 when I first stumbled across a copy of Raymond Moody's 'Life after Life' that memories of that remarkable evening, which had lain dormant in my mind for so many years, came flooding back to rekindle my interest in what he called the 'near death experience, (NDE)'.

The following chapters in this book review the published literature regarding this phenomenon and seek to highlight the salient features from what are now thousands of accounts brought back by those whose life was ' hanging by a thread', but who survived to tell their story.

INTRODUCTION

Death is the destination we all share.

No one has ever escaped it. And that is as it should be because

death is very likely the single best invention of life. (Steve Jobs).

Today, many of us busy ourselves in pursuit of the pleasures of life and give little thought of arriving at our final resting place. However, for past generations journey-times were often short. Death was a frequent interposer, thrusting itself upon the populace, rich and poor, with much greater prevalence than now, at least in the Western world. No surprise then, that a conversation around the subject of death in much of the 20th century assumed the same taboo status as did sex for the Victorians.

However, in 1975 a book was published by Dr. Raymond Moody, an American medical psychologist, which he entitled 'Life after Life'. This publication served to rekindle the subject of dying in the minds of modern day society and was remarkably successful, becoming an instant bestseller. In his book, Moody described the experiences of critically ill patients, many diagnosed by attending physicians as being clinically dead, but who had subsequently made a recovery. The accounts of the events related by these survivors following their 'demise' were found to be remarkably consistent and incorporated distinct temporal stages or events in what Moody called the Near Death Experience (NDE). Subsequently, many more investigations into the

NDE phenomenon by other workers in the medical field have been undertaken, largely verifying Moody's findings. Not everyone experiences each stage of the NDE and variations abound, but they all seem to follow a central pattern.

Unusual or unexpected events observed by those attending a dying person have been well testified for centuries. The so called 'death-bed vision' has been witnessed many times, with the dying person (and occasionally their attendants) speaking of seeing dead relatives and/or angelic figures around them at a time close to death. An intriguing collection of these events can be found in Sir William Barrett's 'Death-Bed Visions, the Psychical Experiences of the Dying', first published in 1926. Barrett was a founder member of the Society of Psychical Research (SPR) formed in 1882 to apply the techniques of stark scientific enquiry to matters formally the province of Spiritualist movements whose reputation had been badly tainted by accusations of fraud.

In Barratt's time, there was little the doctor could do to prevent the inevitable decline of his patient into death and the dying person simply slipped into the next world or oblivion (whichever you believe), never to return. However, with rapid advances in medical knowledge, including modern techniques of resuscitation, large numbers of critically-ill individuals, showing no vital signs, can now literally be brought back from the dead to tell their tale.

Whatever the origin or cause of the NDE, the event is highly significant and influential to those who have been through it and the experience often has a most profound effect regarding their outlook on life following recovery.

Chapter 1

THE CLASSIC NEAR-DEATH EXPERIENCE

Before we explore the NDE in detail, it will be useful to describe a typical, composite event which includes all the major reported features from those who have been close to death but have recovered to tell of their experiences. It should be stressed that not everyone relates all the events described below and, as we will see later, there are many variations around a central theme. Here is my construction of a classic full NDE :-

A man, let's call him John, is admitted to the A&E unit of his local hospital suffering from a severe myocardial infarction. He is rushed on a trolley into a room where medical personnel make an urgent assessment of the patient's condition. During this examination, John's heart goes into ventricular fibrillation and ceases to beat. He falls deeply unconscious.

From the darkness of unconsciousness he suddenly becomes aware that he has regained his senses, but he has become detached from his body. He gazes down on a scene below from a vantage point near to the ceiling. After a moment's confusion it dawns on him that he is looking at himself lying on the trolley, surrounded by a number of attendants who are in a state of agitation. John concludes that his death has come, but thinks nothing of it, he feels no remorse or sadness, indeed he feels positively happy. All pain has disappeared and he feels warm and comfortable; in fact he never felt better in his whole life. John feels alert and highly perceptive. He can't understand what all the fuss is about and wants to tell those tending him that he feels fine and to leave his body alone. He tries to communicate this to the people below, but they seem oblivious to his expostulations. John stays a little longer. He can describe in detail the physical appearance of individual members of the medical team, the equipment present and the sequence of events leading to his attempted resuscitation. He observes his body jumping up a few inches from the bed as the defibrillator electrode pads are applied to his chest. All this fascinates him. John then realizes he can move, he can 'think' himself into different places. He ventures out into the lobby. He sees his wife in a navy blue jacket and black skirt sobbing in the waiting room. She is being comforted by his sister who has her arm around her shoulder and is whispering in her ear. Strangely, John does not share their unhappiness and worry. He is devoid of emotion.

Then he notices that above him appears the entrance to a dark tunnel and he feels himself floating up towards it. The clamour of the hospital fades from his senses. At the end of the tunnel a light appears and grows ever larger as he accelerates towards it. He hears a rushing noise as he travels along at great speed. John stops as he reaches the light which seems so radiant, brighter than the sun, but, despite its intensity, does not hurt his eyes. The light then reveals a beautiful country garden, with flowers of every description and hue, all portrayed in the brightest of colours. There is a pleasant fragrance in the air from all these blooms. Beyond the garden are trees and fields of the most vivid green. The sun shines warmly from a deep blue sky, but strangely no shadows are cast.

Enchanting choral music can be heard in the background and a feeling of bliss overwhelms him.

As he strolls through the garden John sees a fence, beyond which is an assemblage of people waving at him to come closer. He walks over and notices his deceased grandparents are among the group. They appear to look much younger and more vibrant than he remembered them in life. They exchange thoughts without speaking and he is made to feel very welcome. They urge him to climb the fence and join them. However, John instinctively becomes aware that to cross the barrier of the fence would mean his stay in this place would be permanent and he would not be able to return to his earthly body. So enthused with well-being is our patient that he moves closer to the fence in order to surmount it and join the happy throng beyond. As he does so, however, John suddenly becomes aware of an awe-inspiring presence, a supreme being who holds him back. John feels surrounded by love emanating from this brightly shining entity and is asked what he had done with his life on earth. As John starts to explain, he sees before him flashes of his life replayed like movie snippets just as they had happened years earlier, from early childhood onwards. The entity focuses on some of these. In particular, John is shown incidences of his meanness and ingratitude towards others.....the theft of his sister's Easter egg and her resulting unhappiness.....swearing at his mother to deliberately make her upset.....hiding his brother's car keys to make him late for a job interview. John is allowed to appreciate how his actions led to the sorrow and distress of others. All through this life review, the entity is never condemnatory and love and understanding permeate the whole event.

The entity then explains that John cannot stay in this place as he still has things to perform in the earthly realm. John pleads to stay, but the decision has been made and he feels himself descending back through the tunnel. He hears a click and a momentary surge of pain as he re-enters his body on the hospital bed.

A few days later John is told by the cardiac consultant on his rounds that he had had a close call and it was touch and go for a while, but that his heart had now resumed its normal rhythm. John tries to relate some of his remarkable experience to the doctor in search of an explanation. On hearing the patient's description of his own resuscitation, the consultant is baffled by how accurately John has recounted the events inside the assessment room on that fateful day. 'That's the way it was', the doctor says with surprise, 'but there is no way in the world you could have known anything at all about what happened. You were deeply unconscious. Indeed, you were clinically dead. It's impossible!'

The consultant walks slowly away shrugging his shoulders, his eyes to the ground, his mind in deep thought. This is not the first time he has encountered accurate recall in patients showing no vital signs of life. Maybe he'll write a book on the subject.

John is discharged from hospital. His life has taken on new meaning. He has a heightened awareness of the 'hopes and fears' of others around him. He is more attuned to people's feelings and he becomes much less self-orientated. All fear of death has abandoned him.

Now, as mentioned earlier, the above account does not describe the experience of one particular person, but it incorporates the major elements from what are now many thousands of reports from those who have recovered from life-threatening events. It is rare for anyone to tell of an experience as full as that given above. In most, but not all cases, the longer the person remains 'at death's door', the more expansive and comprehensive their experience becomes.

The following chapters review, in turn, each of the main stages of the NDE and seek to provide an explanation for them.

CHAPTER 2

COMPONENT FEATURES
OF THE NEAR-DEATH-EXPERIENCE

1. THE OUT-OF-BODY EXPERIENCE (OBE)

a) <u>Autoscopic descriptions</u>

The first event most often reported by someone undergoing a NDE is an awareness that they have, in some way, become detached from their body and assume a feeling of lightness and buoyancy. Invariably they are situated close to their 'dead' body, usually at a slightly elevated vantage point. This allows them to gain an unimpeded view of the situation around them, which often includes other people in the vicinity who are trying to help. Such scenes are often frenetic as can be imagined. It might be supposed that the sight of one's body *in extremis* and the realization that your life had ended would engender emotions of upset and panic in the percipient. Quite the opposite is true for the NDEer. He / she usually remains impassive and nonchalant about the whole affair. Initially there may be fleeting apprehension or even fear, but very soon, instead of anxiety and stress, feelings of indifference or mild fascination prevail.

For example, following a serious car crash, a girl reports :-

I could see my body all tangled up in the car amongst all the people who had gathered around, but, you know, I had no feelings for it whatsoever. It was like it was a completely different human or maybe just an object......I knew it was my body, but I had no feelings for it. (1)

and

I had a floating sensation as I felt myself get out of my body and I looked back and I could see myself on the bed below and there was no fear. It was quiet, very peaceful and serene. I was not in the least bit upset or frightened. It was just a tranquil feeling and it was something I didn't dread...........(2)

And this account from a woman in Florida who was hit by a speeding car in 1964

.... I was above the whole scene viewing the accident. I was very detached. I think the thing that impressed me the most was that I was devoid of emotion. It was though I was pure intellect. I wasn't frightened. You know it was all very pleasant. I remember seeing my shoe which was crushed under the car....I remember seeing the earring which was smashed .....and I thought, oh no, my new dress is ruined and I wasn't thinking about my body being possibly ruined too.....I don't think the seriousness of the situation dawned on me...... (3)

In a number of cases the person having undergone an out-of-body experience describes having acquired a heightened sense of awareness and observation. Tiny details are picked up on and remembered, for example, the crushed shoe and smashed earring in the case above.

Here is another example involving a woman who went into shock following post-surgical complications :-

Bang, I left! The next thing I was aware of was floating on the ceiling and seeing (the anaesthetist) *down there, with his hat on his head....it was so vivid. I'm very near-sighted by the way........They were hooking me up to a machine that was behind my head and my very first thought was, 'Jesus, I can see! I can't believe it, I can see!' I could read the numbers on the machine behind my head and I was just so thrilled and I thought, 'They gave me back my glasses' . (4)*

In the next case, which was featured in BBC's 'QED' series in 1987 and described by Peter and Elizabeth Fenwick in their book 'Truth in the Light', no-nonsense retired Army major, Derek Scull recalls his experience in hospital following a heart attack in 1978 :-

I was lying there feeling terrible, absolutely my lowest point. I'd never felt so low..... I felt this enormous tension, as though I knew something was going to happen. Then I felt absolutely airy-fairy, as if I was levitating, quite serene, withdrawn from my body. I floated up to the left hand corner of the room. I looked back and saw my own body, lying there with its eyes closed. It didn't seem at all surprising for me to be up there. I could see through the windows at the top of the room into the reception area outside in the ward. Suddenly, I was conscious of my wife standing at the reception desk, talking to someone who was sitting down behind the desk.....She (his wife) *was wearing a bright red trouser-suit. I thought, my God, what an inappropriate time to arrive.....I'm up here and she's down there and there's the body. What's going to happen ?*

The next thing I was conscious of was being back in my bed, I opened my eyes and there sitting beside me was Joan in her red trouser-suit. I wasn't a bit surprised, because I knew she'd arrived. I'd already seen her. (5)

Perhaps Major Scull in his 'hour of need' had summoned up a picture in his mind of his wife wearing a garment which was a favourite of his in her wardrobe. Perhaps his wife often wore that trouser suit. The Fenwicks established that neither was the case. The only reason that Joan had put on that seldomly worn piece of clothing was because she thought the bright colour would help to cheer her husband up.

Another remarkable instance of recall described by a person near to death is reported by cardio-vascular specialist, Dr. Maurice Rawlings, based in Chattanooga, Tennessee. He personally resuscitated a woman who had attempted suicide. In Rawlings' words :-

'Her heart had long since stopped beating, her face had a dark, bluish tinge. The rest of her body had a death pallor. The electrocardiogram showed straight line standstill . She remained in a coma for four days. Because of the dilated pupils, it appeared that brain damage had occurred....She eventually regained all her faculties and returned to work....About the second day after recovery from her coma, I asked her if she remembered anything at all. She said:-
'Oh, I remember you working on me. You took off your brown plaid brown coat and threw it on the floor and then you loosened your tie. I remember your tie had white and brown stripes on it. The nurse who came in to help you looked so worried! I tried to tell her I was all right. You told her to get an Ambu bag (a disposable bag valve mask resuscitator) *and also an intracath* (an intravenous cannulation device)

to start an I.V. Then two men came in with a stretcher. I remember all of that'.

Rawlings, confirming these events peculiar to her resuscitation continues :-

'Recall with me…….she was in deep coma at that particular time and remained in a coma another four days! At the time I took off my brown plaid coat only she and I were in the room and she was clinically dead'. (6)

A prominent researcher into the NDE phenomenon is an Atlanta-based cardiologist, Dr. Michael Sabom. He started out very sceptical of reports from patients describing visionary events when close to death. He believed that they had somehow constructed in their minds a picture of what might have happened to them after hearing fragments of conversation around them at the time of their crisis (hearing being the last sense to be lost when falling into unconsciousness) and amalgamated this with what they might have seen in hospital scenes from films or on TV. He taped one hundred interviews with people who had undergone an out-of-body experience and then checked back through their medical records retrospectively. He was astonished to find that the patients' description of their resuscitation corresponded closely to what actually did occur. He found that patients were correctly reporting events that were unique to their own treatment. In one case, a retired air-force pilot was able to give detailed information of the appearance and use of the defibrillator, including dial settings and discharge rates. In another, a 62 year old retired mechanic was able to describe a series of events, from the rubbing of lubrication gel over the paddles through to accurately relating the various sampling and injection sites on his body. (7)

With most OBEs, the subject is in close proximity to his/her body (usually several feet to several yards away) and remains in this position until either returning to the body or entering the next stage of the NDE when perception of the body and its earthly surroundings are lost. However, there have been a number of reports where people describe themselves being able to move away from the vantage point above their body. They seem to be able to 'think themselves' to a new location, particularly if something catches their 'eye'.

Dr. Kenneth Ring, professor of Psychology at Connecticut University relates the case of a near-death survivor who saw her sister, a hospital worker, being informed of her critical condition in a different part of the hospital to where she lay :-

'I could follow her movements……someone told her what was going on and she came ripping upstairs. I could see her doing it. I could see her coming up the elevator…..she used the emergency elevator…and she told me this afterwards and I shared that with her'.(8)

Here's another case reported by Dr. Michael Sabom of a Florida night-watchman who was close to death :-

'I could see anywhere I wanted to. I could see out in the parking lot, but I was still in the corridor….It was just like I said 'OK what's going on out in the parking lot?' and part of my brain would go over and take a look at what's going on over there and come back and report to me.'(9)

Even if patients in an out-of-body state stay in the room, their gaze is not continuously fixed on their body or indeed the confines of the room. They have the ability to 'take a look around' and from their elevated position are able to notice things impossible to see at ground level. Take this report from another of Ring's patients :-

'From where I was looking, I could look down on this enormous fluorescent light…. and it was so dirty on top of the light….it was filthy and I can remember thinking, 'Got to tell the nurses about that'. I could see what was going on in the cubicle next to mine. We were in a series of cubicles with curtains in between and I could see the woman in the cubicle next to me and she was asleep'. (10)

And another example reported by Peter and Elizabeth Fenwick :-

'I was exhausted and felt I could no longer bear the pain. I fell backwards onto the pillows. And then I seemed to be looking down on myself. I could see all about me and looking over towards the window I could see children playing in the garden next door. Yet this is something I couldn't possibly have seen from my bed. I looked so peaceful and I can't describe the marvellous feeling I felt…'(11)

An even more striking incident involving out-of-body perception was encountered by a German cancer specialist, Dr. Josef Issels at the Ringberg Clinic in Bavaria. He was conducting his morning ward round when he experienced a remarkable event :-

'…..I went into the room of an elderly woman patient close to death. She looked at me and said, 'Doctor, do you know that I can leave my body?' I knew approaching death often produced the most unusual phenomena. 'I will give you proof here and now', said the woman…….'Doctor, if you go to Room 12, you will find a woman writing a letter to her husband. She has just completed the first page. I've just

seen her do it.' She went on to describe in minute detail what she had just seen. I hurried to Room 12, at the end of the ward. The scene inside was exactly the same as the woman had described it, even down to the contents of the letter. I went back to the elderly woman for an explanation. In the time I had gone she had died. It was the first, but not the last time I experienced unusual happenings with seriously ill patients'. (12)

Perhaps the most celebrated case of perception of objects from afar has been documented by Kimberly Clark Sharp who at the time was a social worker at the Harborview Medical Center cardiac care unit (CCU) in Seattle. It relates to a woman called Maria (a migrant worker) who suffered a cardiac arrest. On her recovery, Maria later described a classic OBE, seeing her body and clinicians working feverishly over it. She was then distracted by something over the emergency driveway outside the window and in an instant she had 'thought herself' out there. Maria then said that she had noticed an object on a window-ledge on the third floor of the main hospital block furthest away from the CCU. She described it thus :-

' A man's dark blue tennis shoe, well-worn, scuffed on the left side where the little toe would go. The shoelace was caught under the heel'.

With mixed emotions, Sharp then went from room to room in the suggested location, pressing her face against each window in turn in an effort to locate the shoe. She eventually found it, exactly as described. Intriguingly, the scuffed toe could only be seen from a perspective outside and above the window. (13)

b) **The nature of the extra-corporeal 'self '.**

So how do people describe the structure or nature of their new-found 'self', when they leave their body?

When subsequently relating their story, most OBEers make no reference to the physical appearance of their out-of-body state. They seem to have been too preoccupied with the observation of their earthly selves and surroundings to pay much attention to this aspect. Only when specific questions on this matter are later put to them by researchers do we find some answers. Many subjects find it difficult to find words adequate enough to describe their state, but here are some examples collected by Moody :-

'I didn't think I was just nothing. It was another body….but not another regular body. It's a little bit different. It was not exactly like a human body, but it wasn't any big glob of matter either and I know I still had something you could call hands.'(14)

And :-

'During this time, I kept getting in and out of my physical body and I could see it from directly above. But while I did, I was still in a body, not a physical body, but something I can best describe as an energy pattern. If I had to put it into words, I would say that it was transparent, a spiritual as opposed to a material being. Yet it definitely had different parts.'(15)

And :-

'I still felt an entire body form, legs, arms, everything while I was weightless'. (16)

Other informants were much less specific regarding their appearance, simply alluding to a 'capsule', a 'cloud', an 'energy field', or 'vapour'.

The following examples are interesting, because they describe 'bodily' interactions by the OBEer with individuals who have gathered around their earthly body. For example, this man talking of a car crash :-

'People were walking up from all directions to get to the wreck. I could see them and I was in the middle of a very narrow walkway. Anyway, as they came by, they wouldn't seem to notice me. They would just keep on walking with their eyes straight ahead. As they came real close, I would try to turn around, to get out of their way, but they would just walk through me'. (17)

In both of the next two cases, the OBEer's perception is that he has retained his limbs and that his existence is not simply that of a by-standing blob of pure intellect or a kernel of consciousness :-

'The doctors and nurses were pounding on my body to try to get I.V's started and to get me back and I kept trying to tell them, 'Leave me alone. All I want is to be left alone. Quit pounding on me'. But they didn't hear me. So I tried to move their hands to keep them from pounding on my body, but nothing would happen……It looked like I was touching their hands and I tried to move them, yet when I would give it the stroke, their hands were still there. I didn't know if my hand was going through it, around it, or what. I didn't feel any pressure against their hands when I was trying to move them'.(18)

And :-

'…..I have died, as men termed death and yet I am as much a man as ever…..I recollect distinctly how I appeared to myself, something like a

jelly-fish as regards colour and form……at last I broke loose from the body….where I slowly rose and expanded into the full stature of a man. I seemed to be translucent, of a bluish cast. My elbow came in contact with the arm of one or two gentlemen who were standing by the door. To my surprise his arm passed through mine without apparent resistance, the severed parts closing again without pain as air reunites. I looked quickly up at his face to see if he had noticed the contact, but he gave me no sign, only stood and gazed toward the couch I had just left. I directed my gaze in the direction of his and saw my own dead body…… I was surprised to see the paleness of the face……I saw a number of persons sitting and standing about the body. I now attempted to gain the attention of the people with the object of comforting them as well as assuring them of their own immortality. I bowed to them playfully and saluted with my right hand. I passed among them, also, but found that they gave me no heed….. Only minutes ago I was horribly sick and distressed. Then came that change called death which I have so much dreaded. This has passed now and here I am, still a man, alive and thinking, yes, thinking as clearly as ever and how well I feel …….'(19)

This last account, as can be deduced by the style of the narrative, is an early documented account of an OBE. It dates from 1889, the percipient being a physician, a Dr Wiltse of Kansas. He was being treated for fulminating typhoid fever. His doctor had declared him dead following an incredible four hours without detectable heartbeat and a full thirty minutes without breathing. Wiltse's subsequent recovery was little short of miraculous and, as we shall see later, his experience didn't end here. He has more to tell us. This case was first reported in the November 1889 issue of the St. Louis Medical and Surgical Journal.

Let's finish this section with a quote from pioneering NDE researcher, Raymond Moody, where he concludes that people in their spiritual or astral form are in a unique position :-

'A person in the spiritual body is in a privileged position in relation to the other persons around him. He can see and hear them. (Many a spy would consider this an enviable condition). Likewise, though the doorknob seems to go through his hand when he touches it, it really doesn't matter anyway, because he soon finds that he can just go <u>through</u> the door. Travel, once he gets the hang of it, is exceptionally easy in this state. Physical objects present no barrier and movement from one place to another can be extremely rapid, almost instantaneous '. (20)

2.   THE TUNNEL, THE LIGHT AND THE WORLD BEYOND

a) <u>THE TUNNEL</u>

Perhaps the most well-known of all the events comprising a NDE is the perception of travelling along a long dark tunnel towards a circular bright white light which illuminates the farthest end of it.

This appears to be the next stage following the OBE. Not everyone has this experience, but it is commonly reported.

In the classic NDE, the percipient's attention is drawn away from gazing at the scene of their demise and towards what appears to be the entrance of a dark chasm. They feel themselves drawn into the darkness and the earthly events below disappear. Here are some descriptions :-

'I was in an utterly black, dark void. It was very difficult to explain, but it felt as if I was moving in a vacuum, just through blackness. It was like being in a cylinder which had no air in it. It was a feeling of limbo, of being half-way here and halfway somewhere else'. (21)

In another instance, a woman who lost consciousness after her blood pressure fell dangerously low following a haemorrhage recalls :-

'Against the ceiling beside me was a wide-bore pipe or narrow tunnel, though which I was obviously meant to make my exit and in the distance at the end of it, it seemed to be even brighter.....actually like the sun itself up there. The pipe itself was corrugated or ridged in some way, like the sort of tube you can attach to your tumble dryer.....'(22)

This account is interesting since the informant describes a structure to the tunnel. Another person also relates the appearance of a place she found herself in as being *'a tunnel of concentric circles'* (23). For most, however, the tunnel is described as being 'black' and 'velvety', whist others mention illumination of its interior from the light in the distance.

The reported speed of travel is a very variable feature, some mention being virtually motionless or suspended in the blackness, some describe a slow, pedestrian ascent:-

'I felt as though I left my body and went walking towards a very bright white light at the end of a long tunnel.'(24)

However, the usual description is one of moving at speed, as is given here by a young woman who suffered a severe post-partum haemorrhage :-

'Next I was hurtling down this dark tunnel at high speed, not touching the sides. It made a sort of swishing sound. At the end of the tunnel was this yellow-white light and I said, 'This must be what it feels like to die. I feel no pain at all''. (25)

An intriguing account, from a woman who watched her cardiac resuscitation take place, suggests that she was at the junction of the OBE and 'tunnel' experience, since perception of both occurred simultaneously :-

'I had left my body and was to the side in sort of like a tube. It was real dark in there, but I could see what they were doing. I could hear them. I saw them doing all this stuff to me….. I just slid from the bed right into that tube, just drifted in there…….But around my body it was light, just like a room would be. Whatever I was in, it was black, but I could see out and watch everything' .(26)

Sometimes, the route to the light that people describe is not perceived as a tunnel as such, but is allied to that image and nearly always the welcoming light is seen shining ever more brightly at the end.

For example, one person suddenly became aware of travelling along :-

' a dark country lane with high hedges. At the bottom of the lane there was a cottage with a light in the window.' (27).

Another recalled :-

'During my coma I found myself floating in a valley. There was a light in the distance on a mountain'. (28)

In his collection of interview reports, Moody quotes the following words used by those moving towards the light. They saw themselves as being in *'a cave, a well, a trough, an enclosure, a funnel, a void, a sewer and a cylinder'. (29)*

b) THE LIGHT

The general perception by 'tunnel travellers' is that they are, in some way drawn instinctively or magnetically towards the light, rather than it being a conscious action on their part to move forward. In a very few cases, mention is made of others moving alongside them, usually, it is felt, as guides, soothing their path to the light.

As the end of the tunnel approaches, the traveller pays more attention to the light. Usually it is described as being 'very bright', usually 'white', but the colour has also been described as 'yellow' and occasionally 'orange'. One feature sometimes mentioned is surprise that a light of such great intensity does not hurt their 'eyes' as they gaze upon it. Some even mention putting their 'hands' in front of their 'faces' before realizing that they wouldn't be dazzled. As they move closer, they appear to be enveloped by the light. Two descriptions of the light are as follows :-

'At the end of the tunnel was a glowing light. It looked like an orange --- you've seen the sunset in the afternoon? From the light it makes up an orange glow, with a yellow tint in a circle. That's what it looked like at the ends of the tunnel. I never did reach the end of that tunnel'. (30)

And :-

'The light was really the absence of darkness. We're not used to that concept because we always get a shadow from a light, unless the light is all around us. But this light was so total and complete that you didn't look at the light, you were in the light. See what I'm saying?' (31)

c) <u>THE WORLD BEYOND</u>

Having arrived at the light, the sights and events that follow are described very differently from person to person, though there is a core of consistency and broad themes remain. As they draw closer, the light itself appears to some as a glowing being. Others perceive the light as simply an entrance to another world. In passing through, a sight sometimes reported is that of an enchanting country garden or an idyllic landscape. He are three examples reported by Peter and Elizabeth Fenwick from British patients. (32) :-

'I floated up into a beautiful vivid green field'

And :-

'Suddenly I found myself standing in a field of beautiful yellow corn. The sky on the horizon was the deepest of sky blues that I have ever seen and I felt even more at peace in this lovely tranquil place. The brightness was strong, but not overbearing and I felt comfortable and appeared to be wearing a blue gown.'

And:-

'This was an old-fashioned, typically English country garden, with a lush green velvet lawn, bounded by deep curving borders brimming with flowers…….proclaiming their presence with a riot of colour and fragrance, as if blessed by a morning dew. The entrance to the garden

was marked by a trellis of honeysuckle so laden that you had to crouch down to pass beneath, while at the other end a rustic country gate led to the outside. It was here that my walk through was to end'.

Michael Sabom relates this recollection of a man, living in Texas who suffered a cardiac arrest :-

'I was suspended over a fence....On one side of the fence it was extremely scraggy territory, mosquito brush and generally a junky place you wouldn't want to be. On the other side of the fence was the most beautiful pasture scene I have ever seen in my life or even imagined, in the distance some beautiful trees, beautiful grass and horses. The fence was definitely a dividing line.......The scraggy place is where I live......The other place is where I am going.' (33)

A similar experience was described by a 30 year old New York woman following complications from endometriosis :-

'Suddenly I was aware of being in the most beautiful garden I've ever seen. I felt whole and loved. My sense of well-being was complete. I heard celestial music clearly and saw vivid coloured flowers like nothing seen on Earth, gorgeous greenery and trees.'(34)

As is shown in this last report, the hearing of beautiful music is sometimes reported during a near-death experience. Here is another account :-

'I remember going into a tunnel......I heard beautiful music, something I've never heard before.......I remember coming round in a side ward and asking a nurse where the music came from. She looked at me with a funny look. But there was no music near the room. My husband said that I must have been dreaming, but I know I wasn't.' (35)

In an interesting Victorian account, investigated by the Society for Psychical Research in 1884, we learn nothing about the patient's perceptions, but enchanting music is heard by all but one of six attendants at the bedside of a dying woman. The music that they heard was described by one person present as being *'low, soft music, exceedingly sweet, as of three girls' voices'*, by a second as *'very low sweet singing'* and by a third as *'a few bars of lovely music, not unlike that from an aeolian harp and it filled the air for a few seconds.'* (36)

Though not particularly evidential, it might be worth quoting the report of a very similar event by John Bunyan, the celebrated author of 'The Pilgrim's Progress' and dating from around 1675. In it he refers to a 'godly old puritan' who had recently died in the village :-

'…..This man after a long and godly life fell sick. Of the sickness whereof he died. And, as he lay drawing on, the woman that looked to him thought she heard music and that being the sweetest that ever she heard in her life, which also continued until he gave up the ghost. Now, when his soul departed from him, the music seemed to withdraw and to go further and further off from the house and so it went until the sound was quite gone out of hearing.' (37)

The scent or perfume from flowers growing in the idyllic garden may also be remembered.

'This place was amass with beautiful flowers, the perfume from them was very strong …… I got out of bed to realize all the pain I had had gone. All I had left as proof of this miracle was the perfume of the garden still lingering in my bedroom, which my husband could smell.'(38)

Thus it appears that musical sounds and pleasant aromas from the 'next world' can linger with the patient even after they have fully regained consciousness. Indeed, one patient following her NDE found that she experienced a strong smell of flower perfume when someone close to her was about to die.

Many descriptions of the world beyond that have been given are certainly stereotypes of the popular concepts of heaven. Again, quoting from Dr Sabom's subjects :-

'walking on clouds on a clear, beautiful summer day, with clear sky';

'walking up some steps that I shouldn't have been walking on, which led to the golden gates of heaven'; 'the gates of heaven, with people on the other side'; 'a gold ornamental gate, wrought-iron in appearance, with a highly polished colour.' (39)

Some people, apparently deeper into their experience, tell of seeing buildings or structures of some kind. Take this example from a cardiac-arrest victim:-

'And then I walked through the door and saw on the other side a beautiful, brilliantly lit city, reflecting what seemed to be the sun's rays. It was all made of some shiny metal with domes and steeples in beautiful array and the streets were shining, not quite like marble, but made of something I have never seen before. There were many people all dressed in glowing white robes with radiant faces. They looked beautiful. The air was so fresh. I have never smelled anything like it.'(40)

A similar 'city of light' was described by a man struck by lightning and who subsequently underwent an exceptionally prolonged near-death experience. At the juncture described below, he is accompanied by what he perceives as 'a being of light' :-

'Like wingless birds we swept into a city of cathedrals. These cathedrals were made entirely of a crystalline substance that glowed with light that shone powerfully within. We stood before one.....The walls were made of large glass bricks that glowed from within. These structures were not related to a specific religion of any kind. They were monuments to the glory of God.' (41)

Another patient describes being transported to an ethereal city, following complications in fitting a new pacemaker to his heart :-

'.......A nurse, it seemed, had grasped me from behind, encircling my waist with her arms and took me out there. We started flying out of the city, going faster and faster. The first time I knew it was not a nurse was when I looked down toward my feet and saw the tips of some white wings moving behind me. I am sure now it was an angel. After soaring for a while, she sat me down on a street in a fabulous city of buildings made of glittering gold and silver and beautiful trees. A beautiful light was everywhere-----glowing, but not strong enough to make me squint my eyes.......I don't think anyone could be an atheist if he had an experience like me.' (42)

At the end of his story, the patient describes being returned by the 'angel' to his hospital bed, then gazing up at the faces of the medical staff who were tending him.

d) **THE BARRIER**

Whether at the location of the light itself or in the ethereal world beyond, many people tell of coming across a barrier of some kind, which is described in a variety of different forms. They become aware that this barrier constitutes the boundary between earthly and 'heavenly' existence and that it represents a point of no return. Many try to cross over or through it but feel themselves prevented in doing so.

These three examples are given by the Fenwicks :-

'Inside was the most beautiful garden, no lawn, path or anything else, but flowers of every kind..........I pushed the gates and they gave way to my push, but try as I might I could not get in; there was something behind me on both sides which seemed to be stopping me from going in. I was so upset at not being able to get in, but in the end I gave up trying.'

And*:-*

'As I was going down the slides, I could see a barrier at the bottom. It was like a shiny black leather bench. I knew that if I went over the barrier I would be dead'.

And:-

'I was floating in total blackness when far ahead of me I saw a wrought-iron gate----a tall church window-shaped gate which was open.....I gently floated on towards the gate, then the middle figure looked at me and shook his head, giving me the impression that I wasn't to be allowed in yet, though no words were spoken. '(43)

Again, in a similar vein, this American woman who suffered a cardiac arrest whilst undergoing surgery to remove a brain tumour reports as having been turned back by two spiritual entities :-

'It was life, joy and peace to the fullest you could think of and more. But then there was this barrier. I tried to push it with all my strength, but I couldn't move it. I could see through it, but I couldn't push through it. I knew that if I just stepped over there, I could stay in that light forever. Two mighty angels were standing in the light. They were holding up their hands stopping me. I knew their hands had something to do with the barrier. They didn't say anything. It was just like there was an understanding. My spirit had to turn around and I was ushered back down that dark corridor. I was sad. The next thing I remember, I looked up and there was Gerry (her husband).' (44)

Let us now turn again the 1889 near-death experience of Dr. Wiltse , the typhoid victim, for he too encountered a barrier on 'the road to the eternal world'. He described himself as being lifted and gently propelled through the air by someone's hand and placed on a road in the sky upon which he encountered three :-

'Prodigious rocks blocking the road, at which site I stopped, wondering why so fair a road should be thus blocked and while I considered what I was to do, a great dark cloud, which I compared to a cubic acre in size, stood over my head........I was aware of a presence which I could not see, but which I knew was entering the cloud from the southern side. The presence did not seem, to my mind, as a form because it filled the cloud like some vast intelligence......thoughts not my own entered into my brain .The Being told me 'This is the road to the eternal world. Yonder rocks are the boundary between the two worlds and the two lives. Once you pass them, you can no longer return into the body'.....I was tempted to cross the boundary line......now that I am so near I wanted to cross the line and stay......and advance the left foot across the line. As I did so, a small-density black cloud appeared in front of me and

advanced towards my face. I knew I was to be stopped. I felt the power to move or to think leaving me. My hands felt powerless at my side, my head dropped forward, the cloud touched my face and I knew no more.

Dr Wiltse then describes returning to the scene of his earthly 'death':-

'I was in the body and in astonishment and disappointment, I exclaimed "What in the world has happened to me? Must I die again?" I was extremely weak, but strong enough to relate the above despite all injunctions to be quiet......I made a rapid and good recovery.' (19).

3.   THE MEETING WITH OTHERS

As can be seen from the accounts given in the last chapter, people rarely find themselves alone after the light has been reached. Either at the light itself, or in the world beyond, the near-death traveller usually detects the presence of others. Often, communication between the parties takes place. In its simplest form, all that that is perceived is a gesture; the shake of the head or a wave of an arm from an astral being or even just a nuance given by the light which is intuitively understood. At the other extreme, lengthy dialogue ensues. Quite often this intercourse is described as being *'non-verbal'*, in that the participants seem to be *'able to read each other's minds'*, through *'telepathic transfer of thought'*. Any 'conversation' that takes place is invariably amicable. Those entities which appear may be figures well known to the NDEer or be complete strangers to him / her.

If friends or family are encountered, they seem to instantly recognize the newcomer and extend a welcome. They appear to look happy and in the best of health. Cases have been reported where those crippled in their earthly existence now appear to walk normally, without pain or inconvenience and elderly relatives may look years younger. Sometimes, members of the welcoming party are seen clothed in white robes or shimmering garments of some kind, with a glow or an aura emanating from them. Strangers likewise may be described as 'glowing' or 'shining' and be identified as 'angels', 'heavenly guides' or 'spiritual emissaries'.

Deceased relatives are often encountered. Here is a typical example from a 43 year old man who suffered a post-operative heart seizure :-

'I came to some place and there all my relatives were, my grandmother, my grandfather, my father, my uncle who had recently committed suicide. They all came towards me and greeted me….My grandparents were dressed all in white and they had a hood over their heads…..they looked better than the last time I saw them…..very, very happy…….I held hands with my grandmother……It seemed like I had just come up on them and they raised their heads up and were all happy……..And all of a sudden, they turned their backs on me and walked away and my grandmother looked over her shoulder and she said ' We'll see you later, but not this time''. (45)

Two more examples are given below :-

'Then suddenly I saw my mother, who had died about nine years ago and she was sitting—she always used to sit in her rocker you know—she was smiling and she just sat there looking at me and she said to

me…..'Well, we've been waiting for you. We've been expecting you. Your father's here and we are going to help you''. (46)

And :-

'There was a background music that was beautiful, heavenly music and I saw two figures walking towards me and I immediately recognized them. They were my mother and father, both had died years ago. My mother was an amputee and yet that leg was now restored. She was walking on two legs!' (47)

Whether or not any other figure is met with, there usually comes a point when, suddenly, the arrival of an awe-inspiring presence overwhelms the NDEer. For many of the Christian faith, this entity is named as God or Jesus without hesitation. Others have described it as a *'supreme being'*, a *'radiant, loving force'* or a *'vast intelligence'* which exudes a feeling of unimaginable warmth, comfort and understanding. The Being never reveals its identity; that is for the beholder to deduce and people of different religious faiths report seeing their own deities.

Here are three typical examples. The first is from a heart attack victim who was brought back into his body by a shock from the defibrillator at the precise time he was in contact with a being of light.

'Suddenly I felt relief from my terrible chest pains. Now I felt exhilaration. I can't fully express it. I was floating into an area that looked like heaven. It was wonderfully bright with buildings and streets of gold and I saw a figure, with long hair in a brilliant white robe. A light

radiated all about him. I didn't talk to him. I am sure it was Jesus. As he took my hand, the next thing I remember was a jerking of my body...and then the pain came back. But I was back on Earth again!.......I am not afraid of death. I really am not. I look forward to seeing Jesus again.' (48)

The second is from another cardiac patient who underwent an open heart operation.

'.....I was walking across this wooden bridge over this running beautiful stream of water and on the opposite side ......there was Christ and he was standing with a very white robe. He had jet black hair and a very black short beard. His teeth were extremely white and his eyes were blue, very blue.......He looked different to any pictures I had seen before.....I was not afraid and was very much at peace'. (49)

The third is from a woman rushed to a New Orleans hospital in a coma a few days after giving birth, following blood loss from an undiagnosed retained placenta.

'......Then I was aware of an immense Presence coming towards me, bathed in white, shimmering light that glowed and at times sparkled like diamonds. Everything else seen, the colours, beings, faded into the distance as the Light Being permeated everything. I was being addressed by an overwhelming presence. The joy and ecstasy were intoxicating. It was 'explained' that I could remain there if I wanted; it was a choice I could make......Part of me wanted to remain forever, but I finally realized I didn't want to leave a new baby motherless. I left with sadness and reluctance. Almost instantly I felt re-entry into my body though the silver cord at the top of my head......I heard someone near me say ,'Oh, we've got her back'. I was told I had had two pieces of placenta as large as grapefruits removed'. (50)

This case is interesting because a point was reached when a choice had to be made to stay or return. This is a commonly reported feature. Whatever the nature or duration of the dialogue, there often comes a stage in the liaison when it is felt that a decision has to be made whether to stay in the 'heavenly realm' or return to the earthly body. Decision making is an event reported by nearly three-quarters of the Fenwicks' subjects (51). However, a disparity arises from experience to experience in just who makes this decision. As in the case above, some say it is they who decide. A typical reason given by the NDEer for wanting to return would be *'there is nobody else but me to look after the children'* or *'who would care for my invalid mother if I wasn't there?'*

Here are another two examples :-

'The peace and happiness were overwhelming, but I knew that if I stayed longer I would not return. I then thought of my wife and young child and I knew I had to return'. (52)

And:-

'At the end of the tunnel there was a very bright luminous light and a landscape beyond, very beautiful. As we approached the light, one of the voices said, 'Are you coming or staying?' and I knew that if I went I would die. I thought about it, certainly there was no fear, but I said, 'No, I haven't finished my life yet.' Instantly I was whisked back......and I was in the recovery room and a nurse was saying. 'She's not coming round, she's not coming round-----oh, it's OK, she's all right.'' (53)

Sometimes, reasons to return may be much more prosaic, for example in one case, a woman felt she had to return because she knew that in the kitchen at home there was a large pile of her husband's shirts which needed ironing!

Others NDEers make it quite clear that they had no part in the decision making. They describe being directed by those on the other side to go back, sometimes against their wishes. The return might be justified with a phrase such as *'It's not your time yet. You still have more to do in your life'*. The following are four examples. Firstly from a female social worker who was involved in a serious car crash :-

'Around me, as the tunnel began to lighten, there were presences. They were not people and I didn't see anything, but I was aware of their <u>minds</u>. They were debating whether I should go back. This was what made me feel so safe. I knew that I had absolutely no responsibility to make any decision......I also knew that I could not influence what decision they made, but that whatever it should be it would be right. There was total wisdom and goodness in them......It was as if there were many minds gathered on each side into one.......I didn't know the outcome, but I was intensely interested and peaceful'. (54)

The next case is very similar, but in this instance, figures and voices were perceived :-

' I was aware at this point of muffled voices to my right. I still couldn't move and yet I could see them......I knew they were discussing me........although I couldn't hear what they were saying. They stood close together and seemed to be looking down at something in their hands. One suddenly looked towards me. I didn't know him, but he seemed to have great presence and authority. His face was very serious. He returned to the discussion and then in a beautiful voice, very loud, he said, 'She must go back'. Oh, the terrible feeling. I felt resentment. I

didn't want to go back. I didn't feel they rejected me, because I knew they loved me. It just wasn't for me to decide'. (55)

In the next two accounts, a deceased family member is recognized as the messenger who states that the NDEer should return :-

'Beyond the mist, I could see people and their forms were just like they were on the earth and I saw something which one could take to be buildings. The whole thing was permeated with the most gorgeous light, a living golden, yellow glow………As I approached more closely, I felt certain that I was going through that mist. It was such a wonderful, joyous feeling……Yet it wasn't my time to go through the mist, for instantly, from the other side appeared, my uncle Carl, who had died many years earlier. He blocked my path saying 'Go back. Your work on Earth has not been completed. Go back now.' I didn't want to go back, but I had no choice and immediately I was back in my body. I felt that horrible pain in my chest and heard my little boy crying. 'God, bring my mommy back to me.'' (56)

And :-

'I saw a group of people between me and the light. I knew them. My brother, who had died a few years before, was gesticulating delightedly as I approached. Their faces were so happy and welcoming. Then somehow my mother became detached from the group. She shook her head and waved her hand (rather like a windscreen wiper) and I stopped and I heard the doctor say, 'She's coming round' and I was in my bed and the doctor and my husband were there. My first words to the doctor were, 'Why did you bring me back?'' (57)

Let's look briefly now at how the return to the body is perceived. Most people remember little or nothing about the process of reunification with their body. Occasionally they tell of travelling, with great speed, back down the tunnel. Re-entry is certainly almost instantaneous and in many cases coincides with a particular resuscitative action, such as an electric shock to the chest. Some say they are guided back to their bodies by a companion that they met earlier in the experience. Interestingly the site of re-entry is usually described as 'the head' and in rare cases they report seeing a 'silvery cord' linking them to their body below.

From these accounts and from many others like them, NDEers do not roam around the idyllic world in isolation and often clear images of persons known or unknown become apparent. Despite finding themselves in a strange place and not knowing what will happen to them, feelings of happiness and contentment predominate. The only negative emotion, felt by some, is disappointment at the decision or the instruction to return.

At the start of the NDE there is nearly always the realization that death has occurred. Surprising, therefore, is the lack of remorse for having died. Even stranger is that little thought is given to anxious relatives (who may even be seen in distress autoscopically) during the OBE. Their grief is not reciprocated.
Even those who, later into the NDE, give the reason to return as 'caring for loved ones' seem to base that decision on a sense of duty rather than on a fervent wish to continue with their life *per se.*

Here are two accounts cited by the Fenwicks from those who later looked back at their experiences:-

'I never once thought of my husband or my children, who were quite young then. It all seemed terribly personal, nothing to do with anyone else…….Later I was riddled with guilt because I had not considered my family.'

And :-

'I love my husband dearly and it now seems very strange that there was no 'pull', no regrets at leaving, nothing; only joy and peace'. (58)

As we have seen, the instruction to return, given by an astral figure is sometimes accompanied by the reason that there is something left undone in their lives or there is still a task to complete before it is time for them to permanently leave their earthly lives. Some remain mystified as to just what that task might be. Others, following their experience, find themselves much more naturally disposed towards helping people and give this as a reason for their return. For example :-

'I say God surely was good to me, because I was dead and he let the doctors bring me back for a purpose. The purpose was to help my wife, I think, because she had a drinking problem and I know she just couldn't have made it without me. She is better now though and I really think it had a lot to do with what I went through……' (59)

One woman simply concluded that she was sent back to reassure her husband, before he passed away, that there was a 'Good Lord' and that he should fear nothing from death.

4.   REVIEWING LIFE EVENTS

A feature of some, but by no means all, NDEs is what researchers have called the 'life review'. It involves the playback of events experienced in one's life in the form of a series of quick visual snapshots, usually in chronological order. These flashbacks include not only glimpses of major, well remembered events, but also seemingly trivial occurrences that had long been forgotten. Despite its brevity, those who have experienced the review speak of their ability to muse and ponder over the significance of each of the scenes that are replayed. Some patients have stated that following their recovery they were still able to recall the events of their lives in incredible detail. Quite often, the review is conducted in the presence of what is interpreted as a 'supreme being.'

Here is one woman's account, which is typical :-

'When the light appeared, the first thing he said to me was, 'What do you have to show me that you've done in your life', or something to this effect. That's when the flashbacks started. I thought, 'Gee, what is going on?', because all of a sudden, I was back in my early childhood. From then on, it was like I was walking from the time of my very early life, on through each year of my life, right up to the present.....'

She goes on to describe seeing herself as a little girl playing down by the creek, breaking a much loved toy at her nursery, camping with the Girl Scouts, feeling proud of her academic achievements at junior school, watching her graduation from high school, reliving her college years and viewing events right up until the time of her illness. She continues :-

'The things that flashed back came in the order of my life and they were so vivid. The scenes were just like you walked outside and saw them, completely three-dimensional and in colour. For instance, when I saw myself breaking the toy, I could see all the movements. It wasn't like I was watching it all from my perspective at the time. It was like the little girl I saw was somebody else, in a movie, one little girl among all the other children out there playing on the playground. Yet it was me. I saw myself doing these things as a child and they were the exact same things I had done, because I remember them.'(60)

It is interesting that this account, along with others, describes viewing past events, not through eyes of the percipient, but from the perspective of someone else watching nearby, as if being filmed on a camcorder. Thus it seems that visual recall has not occurred through the sudden release of a direct personal memory that was stored in the brain at the time of the event, but that it has been formulated from an image collected and held by a third party.

Often in the life review there is perception of heightened emotional insight. Some replayed events generate a warm sense of satisfaction, whilst others lead to feelings of sorrow and shame. Past actions deliberately designed to hurt others are highlighted for particular attention. For example :-

'Most things were pleasant to see, some things made me very embarrassed. In fact revulsion and guilt took away any good feelings, making me very sorry for certain things I had said or done. I hadn't just seen what I had done, but I felt and knew the repercussions of my

actions. I felt the injury and pain of those who suffered because of my selfish or inappropriate behaviour.' (61)

Most of those who experience a life review feel that they will not be punished for their 'misdeeds' and that the exercise is designed purely as a method of instruction and enlightenment. To put it simply, they are being shown how to become a better person. There are those, however, who feel that the outcome of the review will determine exactly what 'level' or 'plane' they are destined for in the afterlife :-

'After the life review I spent some time resting and considering the implications of what had happened. I did not feel I had been judged except by myself. There was no denying the facts because they were all there, including my innermost thoughts, emotions and motives. I knew that my life was over and whatever came next would be a direct consequence of not only what I had done in my life, but what I had thought and what had been my true feeling at the time.' (62)

During an exceptionally extended and spiritual NDE, Betty Eadie in her book 'Embraced by the Light'(63) describes entering a room in which was a 'council' of twelve spiritual beings. She was invited by them to review her life, to which she agreed. This is her account :-

......'My life appeared before me in the form of what we might consider extremely well defined holograms, but at tremendous speed. I was astonished that I could understand so much information at such speed....I not only re-experienced my own emotions at each moment, but also what others around me felt. I experienced their thoughts and feelings about me.......Then I saw the disappointment that I had caused others and I cringed as their feelings of disappointment filled me, compounded by my own guilt. I understood all the suffering I had

caused and I felt it……..I saw my own selfishness and my heart cried for relief. How had I been so uncaring? Then in the midst of my pain, I felt the love of the council come over me. They watched my life with understanding and mercy……and I realized that the council was not judging me, I was judging myself.

The council then described what it called the 'ripple effect' of negative emotion. Eadie continues :-

'I saw how I had often wronged people and how they had often turned to others and committed a similar wrong. This chain continued from victim to victim, like a circle of dominoes, until it came back to the start – to me, the offender.'

With reference to other past events in her life, Eadie was then shown how her acts of helpfulness had rippled out in the same way, but this time to positive effect. She had been shown that both spitefulness and kindness were infectious.

Interestingly, the old adage that a drowning person sees their life flash before their eyes has some truth, since near-death from drowning seems to precipitate a greater number of life reviews than from many other life-threatening causes. The reason may lie in the speed at which death approaches. Changes in blood gas concentrations and brain chemistry are usually much slower in drowning than with say an abrupt cardiac seizure. Perhaps this gives 'time' for a life review to take place.

Regarding the frequency of occurrence of a life review during an NDE, results from different researchers are disparate. Some, such as Moody, Ring, Greyson and Noyes and Kletti all found that between a quarter and a third of subjects reported a review, others have found them much less common. Sabom found only two instances from amongst over 100 NDE cases and Blackmore none at all (*64*). It is not clear why this should be. It is certainly a possibility that those who had experienced a particularly guilt-ridden life review, might be much less predisposed to mention its occurrence during an interview with a researcher. This would serve to drive down the number of reported life review occurrences.

5. **VISIONS OF TERROR**

So far, all of the NDEs we have examined have been, at their blandest, thought- provoking, peaceful events and at their most colourful, highly stimulating and blissfully ecstatic. However, as more and more recollections from people close to death have come to light, accounts of horrifying, deeply troubling experiences have surfaced.

Initial NDE studies conducted by Moody (*1*), Ring (*46*) and Sabom (*9*) were devoid of reports of hell-like visions, but cardiologist Maurice Rawlings in his book 'Beyond Death's Door' (*42*), described direct contact with many patients who had undergone terrifying experiences and concluded that 'bad' experiences may be just as common as 'good' ones. One man whom he was attempting to resuscitate by cardiac massage kept drifting in and out of consciousness. In Rawling's words:- *'Each time he regained heartbeat and respiration, the patient screamed, 'I am in Hell!'. He was terrified and pleaded with me to help him......He then issued a very strange plea: 'Don't stop!' You see, the first things most patients I resuscitate tell me as soon as they regain consciousness is, 'Take your hands off my chest; you're hurting me!' I am big and my method of heart massage sometimes fractures ribs. But this patient was telling me, 'Don't stop!'.......He said, 'Don't you understand? I am in Hell. Each time you quit I go back to Hell!''......After several death episodes he finally asked me, 'How do I stay out of Hell?' ......A couple of days later, I approached my patient with pad and pencil in hand for an interview.......At his bedside I asked him to recall what he actually saw in Hell......He said, 'What Hell? I don't recall any Hell'.......Apparently, the experiences were so frightening, so horrible, so painful that his conscious mind could not cope with them and they were subsequently suppressed far into his subconscious.'*

Here is a report from another of Rawling's patients who was badly injured and close to death after an Industrial accident. In stark contrast to the last, this episode was lucidly recalled :-

'I remember (the event) *more clearly than any other thing that has ever happened to me in my lifetime, every detail of every moment, what I saw and what happened during that hour I was gone from this world. I was standing some distance from this burning, turbulent, rolling mass of blue fire. As far as I could see it was just the same. A lake of fire and brimstone......*

He goes on to describe seeing deceased friends from his childhood:-

'We recognized each other, even though we didn't speak. They too were looking and seemed to be perplexed and in deep thought, as if they could not believe what they saw. Their expressions were those of bewilderment and confusion.......I saw another man coming by in front of us. I knew immediately who He was. He had a strong, kind, compassionate face and unafraid. Master of all he saw. It was Jesus Himself. A great hope took hold of me........just before He passed out of

sight, He turned His head and looked directly at me. That is all it took. His look was enough......In seconds I was back, entering my body again.

The feature in this account which relates, quite literally, to the appearance of a 'Saviour' also occurs in other distressing NDEs. At the nadir of the experience, with the patient in the darkest of despair and praying for deliverance, a figure, usually perceived as 'God' or 'Jesus', rescues the tortured soul and brings them out of the hellish environment. Here is another example from a patient whose blood pressure fell dangerously low :-

'I had severe abdominal pains from an inflammatory condition of the pancreas......and my consciousness was slipping. I remember them working on me. I was going through this long tunnel and I was wondering why my feet weren't touching the sides. I seemed to be floating and going very fast. It seemed to be underground. It may have been a cave, but the awfullest eerie sounds were going on. There was an odour of decay.........some of the workers were only half-human, mocking and talking to each other in a language I didn't understand......there was a large person in radiant white clothes that appeared when I called 'Jesus save me!'. He looked at me and I felt the message 'live differently'. I don't remember leaving there or how I got back. There are a lot of other things that may have happened.......Maybe I'm afraid to remember!'

There is often a sense of being transported downwards in a disturbing NDE, which contrasts to a general feeling of ascension during a peaceful event. Movement along a dark tunnel can feature in both types of experience. As we see from the account above, a downward journey is usually perceived by the NDEer as taking them below the Earth's surface. Whilst underground there is often a feeling of increasing heat which becomes unbearably stifling. Encounters with malevolent entities, either human or non-human are frequently spoken of. In the following case, a woman felt she was about to be dragged down into a dark pit :-

'I found myself in a place surrounded by mist. I felt I was in Hell. There was a big pit with vapour coming out and there were arms and hands coming out trying to grab me……..I was terrified that these hands were going to claw hold of me and pull me into the pit with them.' (65)

Rawlings believes that from the direct data he has obtained it is possible to postulate that at least half of NDEs begin as hellish visions and then progress into heavenly scenarios as the event unfolds and that most survivors remember only the pleasant experience.

Not all researchers agree with this contention. Fenwick has found that people who had been through a 'bad' NDE retained vivid, often painful memories of the event. They are also much more reluctant to talk about their ordeal, compared to those who enjoyed a positive experience, though even in this latter group there may be those who feel that telling their story to others would invite ridicule and so remain silent. Fenwick tells of his contact with a woman who described herself as having had a hellish NDE many years previously. She stated that it had haunted her ever since and she then refused to relate any further details about her experience. Another of Fenwick's subjects talked about keeping a 'voluntary silence' about his terrifying experience due to its upsetting nature. Interestingly though he went on to describe his NDE as having some elements of positivity, including emotions of bliss and joy, mingling with visions of terror (*66*). This harks back to Rawling's assertion that many NDEs have components of pain as well as pleasure.

CHAPTER 3

NDEs IN THE PRE-ADOLESCENT POPULATION

The NDEs that we have looked at so far are those reported from individuals of teenage years upwards; but what about children under the age of twelve, do they also report similar events when close to death? The short answer is 'yes'. This pre-adolescent group is of particular interest because, its younger members at least, are much less likely to have become influenced by cultural or religious conditioning which have shaped the lives of the adult population. Young children are also unlikely to have even considered the prospect of their own death. If you like, they are starting with a 'blank canvas'.

Two researchers, Dr. Elizabeth Kubler-Ross and Dr. Melvin Morse have carried out NDE studies, with a specific focus on children (*67*, *68*). Some of their examples which occurred in childhood are given below :-

 A sixty-two year old woman recounts her experience which took place when she was a child of ten, desperately ill with pneumonia :-

'My first remembrance was that I was floating on the ceiling and I was just so, so happy.......Even now, all these years later, I get very overwhelmed at the feeling..........My first thought was,' how mean of them (her parents) *not to tell me about this before......I would have been here much sooner, how mean'. I was only little. And then I began to look around. There were two very big old-fashioned wardrobes in the*

room and I thought, 'Oh, gee, mother doesn't dust the top very well, I can write my name in this, there's lots of dust'. And I was just enjoying bouncing around. I had total movement and there were no restrictions at all and I knew in which direction I was going. And then I looked down and I saw this little figure on the bed and I thought, 'Oh, isn't she little? Aren't I little? That's me'. And that was OK, that was fine. There was just acknowledgement that that was me down there, But, I <u>knew</u> I was really in total 'up here'.

She then describes seeing both her father and mother at her bedside and she makes the decision to return :-

'The experience was real, absolutely real. I knew I was very sick, I knew that little girl down there was very, very white and I knew I had already left her.......Initially I felt total joy, bliss and perfection that I can't put into words, but then there was an overwhelming disappointment at having to return. I remember it very clearly. It's just as clear now as it was then'.

So here we have the experience of a ten year old child, albeit related after many years, which shows all the features of the initial NDE events that have been reported by adults, i.e. becoming detached from one's dying body, remote viewing of the scene below, attention to detail (the dusty wardrobe tops), a feeling of excessive well-being, indifference in observing one's own 'dead' body, being able to move around at will and the extreme reluctance at having to return to one's body.

Here is another example from a boy, just turned eleven who was knocked off his bike after being hit by a speeding car. His account, which was collected three years after his accident also includes later elements of the NDE, in that he is guided through a tunnel and meets others :-

'I don't remember getting hit, but suddenly I was looking down at myself. I saw my body under the bike and my leg was broken and bleeding. I remember looking and seeing my eyes closed. I was above. I was floating about five feet above my body and there were people all around. An ambulance came. I wondered why the people were worried because I was fine.......The ambulance drove off and I was above the ambulance following it.......When I spoke to them (the ambulance crew) nobody heard me, so I knew I was dead.......I looked around and then I was in a tunnel with a bright light at the end. The tunnel seemed to go up and up......When I was going up in the tunnel, two people were helping me.......They told me I would be okay and would take me into the light. I could feel love from them. I didn't see their faces, just shapes in the tunnel. When we got into the light I could see their faces......It was like they were wearing very white robes. Everything was lighted...... I came out the other side of the tunnel. There were a lot of people in the light, but I didn't know any of them. I told them about the accident and they said I had to go back. They said it wasn't my time to die yet, so I had to go back to my father and mother and sister.......I felt everyone loved me there. Everyone was happy. I feel that the light was God.'

Once again, in this account, we have the later stages of the NDE being played out, i.e. the tunnel, the light, the meeting with others, feeling of love and acceptance, the perception of entering into God's presence and a decision having been made to return.

Both accounts above, even though vividly remembered, were retold years after the event and it could be argued that during this protracted period the teller has wittingly or unwittingly embellished their story in some way. However, the next example was recounted by a seven year old girl only days after recovering from a near-drowning incident at her local swimming pool :-

'I was dead. Then I was in the tunnel. It was dark and I was scared. I couldn't walk. Elizabeth appeared and the tunnel became bright. She was tall, with bright yellow hair and we walked to Heaven. Heaven is fun. It was bright and there were lots of flowers'.

She went on to describe meeting many people, including her dead grandparents, her dead maternal aunt and interestingly, she met two women who were introduced to her as *'Heather and Melissa'*, adults waiting to be reborn. She then met the *'Heavenly father and Jesus'* who asked her if she wanted to return to earth. After declining, she was then asked if she would like to see her mother. She agreed and found herself back at the hospital.

These are just three examples, amongst many hundreds from the young, which show that the age of the percipient appears to be immaterial with regard to the expression of the core features of the experience. Of interest in this last account is the naming of three strangers and the observation that two of them were waiting to be reborn. It is rare in adult NDE's for any stranger to reveal their identity. Even family members do not introduce themselves by name and recognition takes place by 'sight' alone. Notice also that the last two accounts above mention the presence of helping entities in the tunnel. Adults sometimes report this feature, but it is uncommon for them to do so. For a child, being carried by, or being led, holding hands with a parent is a regular occurrence and may be a factor in precipitating the appearance of tunnel escorts.

So the next question is whether really young children, ages three and below can undergo a similar experience? If so it would lead to the conclusion that the NDE is independent of the maturation of the brain and the concomitant increase of synaptic neural connections.

Fenwick (69) cites the case of a three year old girl called Amie who has a rare medical condition called reflex anoxic seizure. With this affliction the heart slows and may actually stop for a short time. Although it would appear serious, the condition is not life-threatening *per se,* as the heart soon regains its normal rhythm again. Nevertheless, it can cause periods of unconsciousness, with no lung ventilation and no heartbeat. When Amie passes out, she later tells her mother what had happened. She regularly speaks of leaving her body and floating to the ceiling where she is able to observe with great clarity all that is taking place below her. Her mother is able to corroborate every detail her daughter tells her. Amie has described seeing a warm, bright light, 'like the sun' and she has touched it, but she knows she must not to go into it and that she must go back to Mummy. She describes returning head-first into her body with a click as being *'not very nice'*.

So even here, at the age of three, we have the OBE, remote viewing, the light and the direction to return. Thus, there is strong reason to suppose that even the immature brain has encoded within it all the necessary mechanisms for the NDE to take place.
Can we take things back even further, say to the time of birth? Well, logically, no. Even the very earliest memories reported by a few people start after the first birthday and usually recall of one's first memory

appears between the ages of two and three. There is however an intriguing account of a woman who right the way through her life remembers the scene of her birth. It had been a difficult labour and the doctor arrived to find her 'blue-black all over'. She remembers floating to the ceiling as being 'a nice experience'. She then recalls looking down and seeing her mother in bed holding her and also her sister-in-law. Suddenly she found herself in a dark pit, climbing frantically up the walls. She continues:-

'I had to get past these horrific, horrible, decrepit people who were moaning and trying to grab me with their arms (this is the part that still frightens me). Then I remember going at great speed down a dark tunnel (the horrid, decrepit people were not there) towards a light. Just as I reached the light, however, for some reason I came away from it and that's all I remember.'

She was told much later that the doctor had dipped her in cold water which stimulated her to breathe and she uttered her first cry.

Again we see in this account some core NDE features and the nightmarish vision of being grabbed by horrid, moaning people has been reported by adults who have undergone a hellish NDE. Also, common to many other 'bad' experiences she then leaves the frightening scene and is attracted towards a light. She attributes her withdrawal from the light as being the instant when the doctor dipped her in cold water. Whatever the reason for her distant memory, it has affected her profoundly and she continually seeks to rid herself of what she describes as, *'the burden that I carry around every day, namely the fear of death'*. Had she reached the light, her experience might well have been transformed into one with a much more positive outcome.

With all childhood NDEs, especially those told by individuals of seven and under, it is difficult to explain why they happen at all, since the conceptual awareness of death is absent in this age group. One explanation is that the NDE has some sort of independent reality. Moody has found that a surprising number of children describe themselves as adults during the episode, although they cannot say how they know this. Perhaps the spirit or the soul can indeed leave the earthly body when it ceases to function and is in itself an ageless entity which simply transfers to another world. Perhaps then, like Heather or Melissa it waits to be reborn?

CHAPTER 4

SOME 'SPECIAL' NEAR-DEATH EXPERIENCES

1. Total brain shutdown

It has been the contention of NDE sceptics that somehow the brain of an unconscious person near to death is still able, through residual activity, to gather recountable information. This acquisition if not by sight, could be attained through the detection of sounds and particularly voices of those nearby. Indeed, hearing is recognised as the last sense to be lost as unconsciousness deepens and often much verbal intercourse takes place in the vicinity of the patient in an emergency situation. Can the brain retain audible information and then conjure up a visual representation of events after recovery has taken place ?

In the case cited below, this would appear not to be the case, since it involved a deliberate full shutdown of brain activity prior to an intricate operation to remove a large cerebral aneurism near to the brain stem. On recovery, the patient reported a vivid NDE during which she was able to view proceedings in the operating theatre, followed by contact and communication with dead relatives, one of whom took her back to her body. The full account of this remarkable NDE can be found in

Michael Sabom's book, 'Light and Death' (*70*). A summary is given below:-

In 1991, Pam Reynolds, an American singer/ songwriter from Atlanta, Georgia started to experience bouts of dizziness and speech loss. A CAT scan revealed the aneurism and it was clear to the physicians that an operation was necessary to save her life. Because of the difficulty in accessing the damaged artery, the only way to treat her was to perform a procedure known as 'hypothermic cardiac arrest'. This involved deliberately reducing her core body temperature to around 16 degrees Celsius, stopping her breathing and heartbeat and draining the blood from her head. Before the operation, ear plugs were inserted, her eyes were covered in tape and the brain stem was monitored to ensure no electrical activity was present upon presentation of an audible stimulus. Pam was now clinically dead in its full medical definition.

During the operation, Pam underwent a full NDE. She saw the surgeons around her body from a position aloft. She was able to hear the electric drill used to cut a flap of her skull and to identify its appearance perfectly. She described her 'sight' and 'hearing' as been augmented and more focused than in life. She was able to recall a female voice saying, 'We have a problem. Her arteries are too small'. (It was later confirmed that the doctors first tried to link up the heart-lung machine to the femoral artery in the right leg, but this being so small, they switched catheter insertion to the left leg). Here is Pam's account in her own words :-

'The saw-thing that I hated the sound of looked like an electric

toothbrush and it had a dent in it, a groove at the top where the saw appeared to go into the handle, but it didn't ... And the saw had interchangeable blades, too, but these blades were in what looked like a socket wrench case ... I heard the saw crank up. I didn't see them use it on my head, but I think I heard it being used on something. It was humming at a relatively high pitch and then all of a sudden it went Brrrrrrrr! like that.

There was a sensation like being pulled, but not against your will. I was going on my own accord because I wanted to go. I have different metaphors to try to explain this. It was like the Wizard of Oz - being taken up in a tornado vortex, only you're not spinning around like you've got vertigo. You're very focused and you have a place to go. The feeling was like going up in an elevator real fast. And there was a

sensation, but it wasn't a bodily, physical sensation. It was like a tunnel but it wasn't a tunnel.

At some point very early in the tunnel vortex I became aware of my grandmother calling me. But I didn't hear her call me with my ears ... It was a clearer hearing than with my ears. I trust that sense more than I trust my own ears.

The feeling was that she wanted me to come to her, so I continued with no fear down the shaft. It's a dark shaft that I went through, and at the very end there was this very little tiny pinpoint of light that kept getting bigger and bigger and bigger.

The light was incredibly bright, like sitting in the middle of a light bulb. It was so bright that I put my hands in front of my face fully expecting to see them and I could not. But I knew they were there. Not from a sense of touch. Again, it's terribly hard to explain, but I knew they were there ...

I noticed that as I began to discern different figures in the light - and they were all covered with light, they were light, and had light permeating all around them - they began to form shapes I could recognize and understand. I could see that one of them was my grandmother. I don't know if it was reality or a projection, but I would know my grandmother, the sound of her, anytime, anywhere.

Everyone I saw, looking back on it, fit perfectly into my understanding of what that person looked like at their best during their lives.

I recognized a lot of people. My uncle Gene was there. So was my great-great-Aunt Maggie, who was really a cousin. On Papa's side of the family, my grandfather was there ... They were specifically taking care of me, looking after me.

They would not permit me to go further ... It was communicated to me - that's the best way I know how to say it, because they didn't speak like I'm speaking - that if I went all the way into the light something would happen to me physically. They would be unable to put this me back into the body me, like I had gone too far and they couldn't reconnect. So they wouldn't let me go anywhere or do anything.

I wanted to go into the light, but I also wanted to come back. I had children to be reared. It was like watching a movie on fast-forward on your VCR: You get the general idea, but the individual freeze-frames are not slow enough to get detail.

Then they [deceased relatives] were feeding me. They were not doing this through my mouth, like with food, but they were nourishing me with something. The only way I know how to put it is something sparkly. Sparkles is the image that I get. I definitely recall the sensation of being nurtured and being fed and being made strong. I know it sounds funny, because obviously it wasn't a physical thing, but inside the experience I felt physically strong, ready for whatever.

My grandmother didn't take me back through the tunnel, or even send me back or ask me to go. She just looked up at me. I expected to go with her, but it was communicated to me that she just didn't think she would do that. My uncle said he would do it. He's the one who took me back through the end of the tunnel. Everything was fine. I did want to go.

But then I got to the end of it and saw the thing, my body. I didn't want to get into it ... It looked terrible, like a train wreck. It looked like what it was: dead. I believe it was covered. It scared me and I didn't want to look at it.

It was communicated to me that it was like jumping into a swimming pool. No problem, just jump right into the swimming pool. I didn't want to, but I guess I was late or something because he [the uncle] *pushed me. I felt a definite repelling and at the same time a pulling from the body. The body was pulling and the tunnel was pushing ... It was like diving into a pool of ice water ... It hurt!*

When I came back, they were playing Hotel California and the line was "You can check out anytime you like, but you can never leave." I mentioned [later] to Dr. Brown that that was incredibly insensitive and he told me that I needed to sleep more. [laughter] When I regained consciousness, I was still on the respirator.'

So here is an experience again showing classic NDE events involving autoscopic viewing, movement along a tunnel with a bright light at the end, meeting and communication with deceased relatives, a boundary not to be crossed, a decision made to be sent back and the experience of pain upon re-entry into the body. An interesting and rarely reported feature in Pam's episode is that she was given sustenance of some kind by those whom she met, which she perceived as being a tonic to help her grow stronger.

The medically controlled environment under which this NDE occurred makes this case particularly relevant, since the brain was measurably in total shutdown. Memory systems are especially sensitive to loss of consciousness, yet here and indeed in many other instances, lucidity of recall is astounding. There is no scientific explanation for this phenomenon. It remains a real enigma.

Pam made a good recovery from this operation, but sadly passed away in May, 2010 as a result of heart failure. She has now truly crossed that boundary.

2. NDEs experienced by the congenitally blind

Another area of great interest involves the reported NDEs by those who have been blind since birth. In their book 'Mindsight : Near-Death and Out-of-Body Experiences in the Blind' (71), Kenneth Ring and Sharon Cooper outline more than thirty such cases.

Perhaps the most complete experience cited in their carefully researched two-year study relates to forty-five year old Vicki Umipeg who was badly injured in a car accident. Vicki was blinded from birth due to an excess of oxygen in a hospital incubator which had completely destroyed her optic nerve. Throughout Vicki's experience, she had no appreciation of colour, but she recalls images of light which were new to her. Her first impression was that of floating above her body and looking downwards :-

'I knew it was me......I was pretty thin then. I was quite tall and thin at that point. And I recognised at first it was a body, but I didn't know it was mine initially.

Then I perceived that I was up on the ceiling and thought, 'Well, that's kind of weird. What am I doing up here ?'. I thought, 'Well that must be me. Am I dead ?'.....

I think I was wearing the plain gold band on my right ring finger and my father's wedding ring next to it. But my wedding ring I definitely saw.... That was the one I noticed the most because it's most unusual. It has orange blossoms on the corner of it'.

Vicki then experienced a rapid upward movement through the hospital roof and could briefly survey a panoramic scene of the environs. Her new-found freedom she found exhilarating. She became aware of exquisite music akin to that made by wind-chimes.

She then experienced being drawn through a tunnel with a light at the end of it, the music changing to that of hymn singing and she found herself in an idyllic pastoral setting, surrounded by many people.

'Everybody there was made of light and I was made of light. What the light conveyed was love. There was love everywhere. It was like love came from the grass, love came from the trees, love came from the birds'.

Vicki then became intuitively aware of specific people she had known who were welcoming her to this place. Among them were two former school friends who had died before their teenage years. They had been profoundly retarded as well as blind, yet here they were happy, healthy and in the prime of life. Her deceased grandmother was also there. Suddenly she became aware of a being of greater radiance than all the others whom she identifies as Jesus. He speaks to her telepathically :-

'Isn't it wonderful ? Everything is beautiful here and it fits together. And you'll find that, but you can't stay here now. It's not your time to be here yet and you have to go back'.

Vicki protests, she wants to stay, but the glowing entity is insistent saying she has more to learn about loving and forgiving and has yet to have her children (she subsequently bore three). Vicki consents, but before she leaves she is given a review of her life and is gently shown the consequences and ramifications of her attitudes and behaviour towards others.

Vicki then returns to her body with what she describes as, *'a sickening thud'*.

The sudden onset of visual perception was somewhat disconcerting to many of these blind subjects. Vicki herself said :-

'I had a real difficult time relating to it (i.e. being able to see) *because I've never experienced it and it was something very foreign to me......It was like hearing words and not being able to understand them, but knowing that they were words. and before you'd never heard anything. But it was something new, something you'd not been able to previously attach any meaning to.'*

Although this was the most detailed NDE related by the blind people in Ring and Cooper's study, some 80% of respondents reported some degree of visual perception during their near-death or out-of-body encounters. The authors have attached the term 'mindsight' to explain how a brain, ever deprived of optical stimuli, is able to achieve a visual awareness which involves ' seeing' in detail, sometimes from all angles at once, with everything in focus, together with a sense of understanding, not just visually, but with multisensory knowledge.

The high percentage (80%) of congenitally blind people reporting visual NDEs / OBEs compared to the sighted population is interesting. People blind from birth are indeed able to dream, but such dreams are played out around emotion, and the senses of touch, hearing, smell and taste since these aspects form a significant part of their waking lives. Visual imagery never features in their dream state.

Another example reported by Ring and Cooper is that of Brad Burrows from Connecticut. Blind from birth and at the age of eight, he suffered a severe attack of pneumonia and was unable to breathe. He recalls seeing himself from above and watching his room-mate run for help, the ascending up through the roof of the building and viewing the city below. He gave a particularly vivid account of the snowy scene below, including the roads cleared free of snow by the ploughs and the heaped masses of snow by the roadside. He saw a street car go by. He was able to recognise his school playground and a particular hill he used to climb nearby:-

'I clearly visualised them. I could suddenly notice them and see them. I remember being able to see quite clearly.'

Brad then goes on to describe the classic passage through a tunnel and arrival at some kind of garden. He was puzzled what to make of his new found sight, but he could 'see' in this domain too and describes a path, tall grass and trees with huge leaves. Everywhere was well lit, but no shadows were cast. He heard wondrous music emanating from a shimmering stone structure which he entered. Here he met an entity who spoke no words, but who gently nudged him backwards. This action precipitated a reversal of Brad's experience and he found himself back in a bed, gasping for air and flanked by two nurses.

Stanislav Grof, in his publication 'Books of the Dead' (*72*), makes an apt summary, even before the promulgation of Ring and Cooper's carefully controlled study :-

'There are....reported cases where individuals who were blind because of medically confirmed damage to their optical system, could at the time of clinical death see the environment. Occurrences of this kind, unlike most of the other aspects of near-death phenomena, can be subjected to objective verification. They thus represent the most convincing proof that what happens in near-death experiences is more than hallucinatory phantasmagoria of physiologically impaired brains.

CHAPTER 5

THE 'AFTERGLOW'

The vast majority of people who have undergone an NDE feel that the event has left with them an enduring legacy in that they now view their lives from a different perspective. In particular, their attitude towards death changes from one of dread and foreboding to, at worst, calm resignation and at best a pleasant anticipation of their final demise. This isn't to say that NDEers want to die; on the contrary, they often proceed to lead fruitful, fulfilling and happy lives, but the most apparent sentiment 'brought back' from an NDE is <u>the loss of the fear of death</u>, which is often associated with the conviction that there is an afterlife.

Here are some typical comments:-

'Everyone's fearful of death, because of the unknown. But if what happened to me is a forerunner of death, then death won't worry me when my time comes.' (73)

'I'm certainly not afraid of dying. I'm pleased in a way, I was given a preview. The experience has had a lasting effect upon my life…..I have no fear when my time for dying comes. I look forward to it with expectation of that wonderful joy and peace.' (74)

and,

'Life is like imprisonment In this state, we just cannot understand what prisons these bodies are. Death is such a release - like an escape from prison. That's the best thing I can think of to compare it to.'(75)

An interesting study has been conducted by Pim Van Lommel and his colleagues in the Netherlands (76). In follow-up research he interviewed a set of near-death patients 2 years after their respective medical crises. This set comprised a near 50/50 split between those who had experienced an NDE and those who had not. Comparative responses between the two groups were analysed using two-tailed statistical models, with their significance identified by p values of less than 0.05. Questions were designed to draw up a 'life-change inventory' for those who had undergone an NDE compared to those who had not. For every feature below, responses from the NDE group were statistically higher. They are given in order of significance (highest first).

1. Appreciation of ordinary things $p = 0.0001$

2. More loving / empathic $p = 0.002$

3. Understanding others $p = 0.003$

4. Belief in life after death $p = 0.007$

5. Involvement in family $p = 0.008$

6. Loss of fear of death $p = 0.009$

7. Acceptance of others $p = 0.012$

8. Understanding oneself $p = 0.019$

9. Interest in the meaning of life $p = 0.020$

10. Understanding the purpose of life   p= 0.020

11. Sense inner meaning of life   p= 0.028

12. Showing own feelings   p= 0.034

13. Interest in Spirituality   p= 0.035

Despite these seemingly positive changes, Van Lommel found that people who had undergone an NDE had a much more complex coping process. They had become more emotionally vulnerable and empathic and there was evidence of increased intuitive feelings. Such heightened awareness was sometimes not easy to deal with, although comfort was derived from lack of the fear of death and a strong belief in the afterlife. In the same study, it was found that after 8 years, survivors could still recall events of their experience almost exactly and the depths of impression were more apparent at 8 years than at the 2 year follow-up. It is remarkable just how indelible the memory of a near-death event proves itself to be.

CHAPTER 6

SOME CELEBRITY NDEs

Those with celebrity status attract the interest of the majority of the general public. Every minutia of personal detail is avidly devoured by the devotee of the revered star. Less well known than the film appearances, the tangled love relationships and the glitzy fashion accoutrements is the fact that these media embedded icons are just as likely to experience a near-death vision as either you or me.

1. **Elizabeth Taylor**.

Elizabeth Taylor was born in London in 1932 to wealthy, socially prominent American parents. She moved to Los Angeles in 1939 and began her career as a child actress in the early 1940s. Taylor starred in many successful films, culminating in 'Cleopatra' (1963) alongside her 5th husband, Richard Burton. Throughout her life, Taylor was prone to illness and injury and in 1961 she survived a near-fatal bout of pneumonia which required a tracheotomy (77). It was at this time, during surgery, that she later described meeting up with her 3rd husband, Mike Todd who had been killed in an aircraft crash in 1958. Todd told her '*No baby, you have to turn around and go back, because there is something very important for you to do. You cannot give up now'.* She felt it was her late husband's love that had brought her back to life (78).

2. **Peter Sellars**.

Peter Sellars was a British actor, comedian and singer, born in 1925. He is, perhaps, best known for his performances in the BBC radio comedy series 'The Goon Show' and as Chief Inspector Clouseau in the 'Pink Panther' series of films. He suffered a series of heart attacks, which eventually led to his death in 1980. During one such event, Sellars described floating out of his body, which allowed him to watch the doctors working on him below his vantage point.

In his own words :-

'Well, I felt myself leave my body. I just floated out of my physical form and I saw them cart my body away to the hospital. I went with it ... I wasn't frightened or anything like that because I was fine; and it was my body that was in trouble. I looked around myself and I saw an incredibly beautiful bright loving white light above me. I wanted to go to that white light more than anything. I've never wanted anything more. I know there was love, real love, on the other side of the light which was attracting me so much. It was kind and loving and I remember thinking 'That's God'. Then I saw a hand reach through the light. I tried to touch it, to grab onto it, to clasp it so it could sweep me up and pull me through it.' (79)

When, presumably, the doctors had succeeded in restarting Sellar's heart, he heard a voice telling him *'It's not time. Go back and finish. It's not time'.* Like many others, when Sellars had regained full consciousness, he expressed disappointment at not being able to pass through the light and revealed how the experience had led him not to fear death.

3. **Donald Sutherland**

Donald Sutherland (born 1935) is a Canadian actor, with a film career spanning six decades. He first rose to fame in the film 'The Dirty Dozen' (1967). He is father of the actor Kiefer Sutherland.

Sutherland experienced an NDE whist filming 'Kelly's Heroes'(1970). He became seriously ill after contracting meningitis. Sutherland explains his experience :-

'Suddenly the pain, fever and acute distress seemed to evaporate. I was floating above my body, surrounded by soft blue light. I began to glide down a long tunnel, away from the bed ... but suddenly I found myself back in my body. The doctors told me later that I had actually died for a time.' (80)

4. **George Foreman**

George Foreman (born 1949) is an American former professional boxer, having won the world heavyweight championship twice. In 1977 Foreman left the ring after a gruelling 12 round contest in Puerto Rico and then collapsed in his dressing room. His subsequent NDE is interesting because it begins with the rare horrific type of experience and ends with his spiritual salvation. His vision left such a deep impression that Foreman subsequently became an ordained minister, initially preaching on street corners before becoming the reverend at The Church of the Lord Jesus Christ in Houston.

In his own words :-

' I was suspended in emptiness, with nothing over my head or under my feet ... This was a place of total isolation, cut off from everything and everyone ... It can only be described as a vacant space of extreme hopelessness ... I knew I was dead, and this wasn't heaven ... Sorrow beyond description engulfed my soul, more than anyone could ever imagine ... If you multiplied every disturbing and frightening thought that you've ever had during your entire life, that wouldn't come close to the panic I felt ... Although I couldn't see anyone, I was aware of other people in this terrible place -- The place reeked with the putrid smell of death ... This place was a vacuum without light, love, or happiness ... In that place, I had no hope for tomorrow -- or of ever getting out.' (81)

He then shouted out :-

"I don't care if this is death. I still believe there's a God!"

Foreman then describes a gigantic hand reaching down and pulling him out of the dark void and being in the presence of Jesus Christ. He awoke with great joy. He later quipped that his opponent had 'knocked the devil out of him'.

5. Jane Seymour OBE

Jane Seymour (born 1951) is a British-American actress, best known for her performances in the James Bond film 'Live and Let Die' (1973), 'East of Eden' (1981) and as Marie Antoinette in the 1989 political thriller 'La Revolution Francaise'. More recently she starred in the American television series ' Dr. Quinn, Medicine woman' (1993-1998).

When she was 36, she had a severe bout of 'flu and was given an injection of penicillin. She suffered an severe allergic reaction which led to her NDE. In her own words :-

'I had anaphylactic shock. It was from an injection I was given when I was playing Maria Callas in the Onassis film. I was in Spain. Routinely, there, when you have very severe bronchitis and they want to give you a major dose of antibiotic, they give it by injection. It was interesting because I remember I felt no pain. I felt no anxiety, but I did feel I needed to go back in that body.

I literally left my body. I had this feeling that I could see myself on the bed, with people grouped around me. I remember them all trying to resuscitate me. I was above them, in the corner of the room looking down. I saw people putting needles in me, trying to hold me down, doing things. I remember my whole life flashing before my eyes, but I wasn't thinking about winning Emmys or anything like that. The only thing I cared about was that I wanted to live because I did not want anyone else looking after my children. I was floating up there thinking, "No, I don't want to die. I'm not ready to leave my kids." And that was when I said to God, "If you're there, God, if you really exist and I survive, I will never take your name in vain again." Although I believe that I "died" for about thirty seconds, I can remember pleading with the doctor to bring me back. I was determined I wasn't going to die."

"I realized you take nothing with you. After that, I also very clearly realized I never wanted to be in debt. So if I had to live on a lot less or I had to live on next to nothing, I would find a way to do that. I realized the only thing I took with me (or almost took with me) when I was passing through were my relationships. But all I wanted was to be able to raise my children and I wanted to feel that I had contributed in some way to the world. I wasn't sure how that was going to be, but I just wanted to come back and participate. I wasn't ready to leave yet.' (82)

6. **Sharon Stone.**

Sharon Stone (born 1958) is an American actress, film producer and former fashion model. She came to public notice for her role opposite Arnold Schwarzennegger in the sci-fi thriller 'Total Recall ' in 1990.

In 2001, she suffered a severe brain haemorrhage and it was while the doctors performed an MRI scan on her, she slipped into unconsciousness. She later described her experience as :-

"It's sort of like passing out but you sort of pass up....... It's just a lot of white light and you see people that have passed on, and they talk to you, and then you pop right back into your body. I felt an incredible sense of well-being....there's nothing to be afraid of.

I had a real journey with this, that took me to places both here and beyond that affected me so profoundly, that my life will never be the same ... I get to be not afraid of dying and I get to tell other people that it's a fabulous thing and that death is a gift. And not that you should kill yourself, but that when death comes to you, as it will, that it's a glorious and beautiful thing. This kind of giant vortex of white light was upon me and I kind of -- poof! Sort of took off into this glorious, bright, bright, bright white light and I started to see and be met by some of my friends. But it was very fast -- whoosh! Suddenly, I was back. I was in my body and I was in the room."(83)

This list of examples of NDE encounters from well known people is by no means exhaustive. Other experiencers include actors Tracy Morgan Robert Pastorelli, Gary Busey , Larry Hagman and Ronald Reagan.

CHAPTER 7

THE SHARED - DEATH EXPERIENCE

The 'shared death experience' is a remarkable event that has been recorded in the literature many times. This phenomenon is experienced by those who are themselves in no way close to death, but who are in close proximity to a dying person. Typically this happens to a healthy individual who is rendering assistance to someone who is dying, sometimes as a result of a sudden or unforeseen circumstance. Thus, the healthy carer somehow becomes enmeshed in and is cognisant of the NDE of the dying person.

Here is an account given by Morse in his book 'Parting Visions' (*84*) :-

'Karl Skala was one of Germany's most noted poets. During World War II, he had an NDE. He and his best friend were huddled together in a foxhole during an artillery bombardment. The shells hit closer and closer until one finally hit close to Skala's friend and killed him. Karl felt his friend slump forward into his arms and go limp with death. Then a strange thing happened to Skala. He states that he felt himself being drawn up with his friend, above their bodies and then above the battlefield. Skala could look down and see himself holding his friend. Then he looked up and saw a bright light and felt himself going toward it with his friend. Then he stopped and returned to his body. He was uninjured except for a hearing loss that resulted from the artillery blast.'

The following account, (85) is from a woman who experienced a vivid, shared life review with her dying husband named Johnny and included events in Johnny early life that she was totally unaware of :-

'I was beside him the whole time in the hospital and was holding onto him when he died. When he did, he went right through my body. It felt like an electric sensation, like when you get your finger in the electrical socket, only much more gentle.

Anyway, when that happened our whole life sprang up around us and just kind of swallowed up the hospital room and everything in it in an instant. There was light all around: a bright, white light that I immediately knew - and Johnny knew - was Christ.

Everything we ever did was there in that light. Plus I saw things about Johnny... I saw him doing things before we were married. You might think that some of it might be embarrassing or personal, and it was. But there was no need for privacy, as strange as that might seem. These were things that Johnny did before we were married. Still, I saw him with girls when he was very young. Later I searched for them in his high school yearbook and was able to find them, just based on what I saw during the life review during his death.

In the middle of this life review, I saw myself there holding onto his dead body, which didn't make me feel bad because he was also completely alive, right beside me, viewing our life together. "Then, right in the middle of this review, the child that we lost to a miscarriage when I was still a teenager stepped forth and embraced us. She was not a figure of a person exactly as you would see a human being, but more the outline or sweet, loving presence of a little girl. The upshot of her being there was that any issues we ever had regarding her loss were made whole and resolved.'

It is interesting that the spirit of an unborn child, lost through miscarriage, appears in this account, as other NDEers have reported seeing images of children they understand to be their own, but that were lost *in utero* and of whom they had no physical recollection. It appears that 'soul acquisition' starts at conception.

Another of Moody's documented accounts (84) concerns a woman in her seventies who described a shared-death-experience whist tending her dying mother. As her mother died, the light in her room suddenly became brighter and she felt a rocking motion spread through her body:-

'This rocking forward motion was very comfortable, and not at all like a shudder and especially not like when a car you are riding in lurches to the side and you get nauseous. I did not feel uncomfortable but in fact the opposite; I felt far more comfortable and peaceful than I ever felt in my life.

I don't know whether I was out of my body or not because all the other things that were going on held my attention. I was just glued to scenes from my mother's life that were flashing throughout the room or around the bed. I cannot even tell whether the room was there any more or if it was, there was a whole section of it I hadn't noticed before. I would compare it to the surprise you would have if you had lived in the same house for many years, but one day you opened up at it and found a big secret compartment you didn't know about. This thing seemed so strange and yet perfectly natural at the same time.

The scenes that were flashing around in midair contained things that had happened to my mother, some of which I remembered and others that I didn't. I could see her looking at the scenes too, and she sure recognized all of them, as I could tell by her expression as she watched. This all happened at once so there is no way of telling it that matches the situation.

The scenes of my mother's life reminded me of old-fashioned flashbulbs going off. When they did, I saw scenes of her life like in one of the 3-D movies of the 1950s.

By the time the flashes of her life were going on, she was out of her body. I saw my father, who passed seven years before, standing there where the head of the bed would have been. By this point the bed was kind of irrelevant and my father was coaching my mother out of the body. I looked right into his face and a recognition of love passed between us, but he went right back to focusing on my mother. He looked like a young man, although he was 79 when he died. There was a glow about or all through him - very vibrant. He was full of life'.

Shared-death accounts come from a variety of sources : soldiers watching comrades die on the battlefield, those holding bedside vigils and people involved in car accidents, where they remain unscathed, whereas another passenger dies.

The following extract describes the experience of a voluntary hospice worker (86):-

'William Peters was working as a volunteer in a hospice when he had a strange encounter with a dying man that changed his life.

The man's name was Ron, and he was a former Merchant Marine who was afflicted with stomach cancer. Peters says he would spend up to three hours a day at Ron's bedside, talking to and reading adventure stories to him because few family or friends visited.

When Peters plopped by Ron's beside around lunch one day, the frail man was semi-conscious. Peters read passages from Jack London's "Call of the Wild" as the frail man struggled to hang on. What happened next, Peters says, was inexplicable.

Peters says he felt a force jerk his spirit upward, out of his body. He floated above Ron's bedside, looking down at the dying man. Then he glanced next to him to discover Ron floating alongside him, looking at the same scene below.

He looked at me and he gave me this happy, contented look as if he was telling me, 'Check this out. Here we are.'

Peters says he then felt his spirit drop into his body again. The experience was over in a flash. Ron died soon afterward, but Peters' questions about that day lingered. He didn't know what to call that moment but he eventually learned that it wasn't unique. Peters had a shared-death experience.

To a person who shares an NDE event there come a number of benefits. Most frequently there is a dramatic reduction in grief which comes from knowing the one who has died is actually existing happily in the afterlife. Secondly there is a greatly reduced fear and apprehension of death and an increased belief in a world to come. Thirdly it provides a deeper understanding and refocusing on one's purpose in this life.

The sceptic would argue that in highly charged environments, such as those described above, there is no shared experience, only hallucinations conjured up by the brain to provide comfort and relief from a highly stressful situation.

CHAPTER 8

CULTURAL ASPECTS TO NDEs

Most NDE research has originated from Europe and the USA. Thus, the majority population, if not strict adherents to Christianity are at least aware of the Christian ethos. But what about other cultures from around the world ?

1. Hinduism

Hindus believe in one God, Brahman, but Brahman can take many guises which means there are literally thousands of gods and goddesses that each contain a part of, or embody a characteristic of Brahman. As far as life after death is concerned there are parallels with Christianity in the belief of Heaven and Hell, though Hindus believe in many planes of afterlife existence and that the soul can move from plane to plane. The spirit may stay in some hellish worlds before moving to heavenly realms or *vice versa*, eventually to be reincarnated. A person's essence can be reborn in a human or animal form. Which direction the next incarnation takes depends on karma. If a person has lived a good life and performed more good deeds than bad, they are reborn into a more fortunate existence. The ultimate goal for a Hindu, after living many lifetimes, is to be released from rebirth and to achieve moksha ; becoming one with Brahman. Hinduism is the world's oldest religion, the roots of which can be traced back over 8000 years.

Some relevant studies have been carried out by Pasricha and Stevenson (*87*). Their findings detail many instances of NDEs reported by people of the Hindu faith, Here are some examples :-

Thirty four year old Chhajju Bania fell ill with a fever and his condition deteriorated to the point where he was thought to have died. His relatives began preparing his body for cremation. However, he again showed signs of life and lived to tell his tale :-

'Four black messengers came and held me. I asked, 'Where are you taking me ? ' They took me and seated me near the God. My body had become small. There was an old lady sitting there. She had a pen in her hand and the clerks had a heap of books in front of them. I was summoned. One of the clerks said, 'We don't need Chhajju Bania (the trader). We had asked for Chhajju Kumhar (the potter). Push him back and bring the other man, he has some life remaining.'. I asked the clerks to give me some work to do and not to send me back. Yamraj (Hindu God of the Dead) *was sitting there on a high chair with a white beard and wearing yellow clothes. He asked me, 'What do you want ?'. I told him that I wanted to stay there. He asked me extend my hand. I don't remember whether he gave me something or not. Then I was pushed down and revived'.*

Chaajju Bania mentioned that he later learned that a person named Chhajju Kumhar had died about the same time that he revived. His behaviour changed following his NDE, particularly in the direction of being more honest.

Another account of a similar theme was described by Vasudev Pandey who had nearly died at the age of ten from what he described as 'parathyphoid disease'. Vasudev was considered dead by relatives and taken to the cremation ground, before some indications of life became manifest. He was immediately taken to hospital where doctors eventually managed to revive him after three days of unconsciousness. He later recalled the following events :-

'Two persons caught me and took me with them. I felt tired after walking some distance ; they started to drag me. My feet became useless. There was a man sitting up. He looked dreadful and was all black. He was not wearing any clothes. He said, in rage, to those who brought me there, ' I asked you to bring Vasudev the gardener. Our garden is drying up. You have brought me Vasudev the student'. When I regained consciousness, Vasudev the gardener was standing in front of me (apparently in group of people around his hospital bed to whom Vasudev, the student, related his experience). *He was hale and hearty. People started teasing him saying, 'now it is your turn'. He seemed to sleep well in the night, but the next morning he was dead'.*

Vasudev Pandey later related that the 'black man', whom he identified as Yamraj, had a club and used foul language. He said that he was brought back by the same two men that had taken him to Yamraj in the first place.

Time and time again, in NDEs from those of the Hindu faith we see references of being taken by messengers, often in an unceremonious manner, to meet an authority figure (usually identified as Yamraj). This rather unpleasant individual, or his functionaries then become frustrated or angry with the messengers, because when lists or records are checked, they find that the messengers have brought the wrong person. The person they were expecting has the same, or a similar name, so the individual taken in error is sent back to resume his / her earthly existence, as their time has not yet come. Meanwhile, the messengers resume their search for the correct entity.

Parallels with 'Western' NDEs include being transported to an unearthly place, meeting with a mystical being, being told they cannot stay as there are still things to do in life and then being taken back to their body.

However, in Hindus' NDEs, very little, if any reference is made to autoscopic viewing of scenes surrounding their 'dead' body. The subject does not look down on his or her physical body as a prelude to deeper experiences. Also, it is not common for Hindus to describe travel through a tunnel or to see a bright light. This is surprising, since, as we have seen earlier, there is a well accepted model to explain these events brought about through oxygen deprivation and there is no reason to suppose any physiological difference between the brain of a devout Hindu and a practicing Christian.

Another disparate feature between Indian and 'Western' NDEs concerns the meeting with other people. Although both cultures commonly describe the presence of a powerful religious, or mystical figure, it is rare in Indian NDEs for a person, at the point of death, to meet identifiable deceased family members; other entities are present, but they are strangers (88, 89). Does this mean that when a person from India dies, random souls are assigned to take that person into the afterlife, whilst a dying American is privileged to be guided by recognisable close family members ? This jars with the notion of a shared afterlife which should be largely the same for all people, whatever their cultural backgrounds.

2. Islam

Originating in Mecca, Islam began in the early 7th century. It is the world's fastest growing major religion with over 1.7 billion Muslim followers. Islam is strictly monotheistic, professing that there is only one incomparable God, Allah, and that Muhammad was the last messenger of God's word. The primary scriptures of Islam are contained in the Qur'an (Koran), which are regarded by Muslims as the verbatim word of God as passed down to Muhammad through the angel Gabriel. Islamists believe that when humans die, their souls remain dormant in an inter-world for a long period of time, waiting for the day of Resurrection / Judgement. When this arrives, the souls rejoin with their bodies and are assigned eternal life, either in Paradise or in the fires of Hell, depending on how righteous or how wicked their lives had been.

Despite the large world-wide population of Muslims, there are very few reported NDEs from this group.

Joel Ibrahim Kreps, a psychiatrist based in Montreal, aware of the dearth of Muslims reporting NDEs, advertised in the traditional media and appropriate Internet groups for Muslims to come forward and relate any personal NDE event. No replies were received. He then commissioned a survey among survivors of the major 2005 earthquake in Pakistani Kashmir. This was conducted by a local university-trained research assistant and a teacher proficient in the local idiomatic language. The study drew a complete blank ; not a single NDE account was forthcoming. Even a doctor, who had personally resuscitated a number of critically ill patients, found no evidence of any NDE recall when he later interviewed them (90). These findings are baffling, since a similar follow-up study among earthquake victims of the 1976 Tangshan earthquake in China revealed that 40% of the 81 survivors who were interviewed reported NDEs (91).

It may be that Muslims do in fact have NDEs, but are reluctant to disclose their experience, since others may consider them heretics if they describe events outside of traditional Islamic beliefs. However Kreps, in his study, relates that the researchers on the ground found that 'the majority of the victims were open and trusting and recounted exactly what they remembered'. He goes on to assert that because Western society has become more secular and religion plays a lesser part in people's lives, an NDE gives the dying person the necessary insight into both the purpose of life and our ultimate destination. 'Pakistani Muslims, however, did not need this type of message. They were already believers in their own revelation, the Qur'an and the tragic events around them served only to confirm their faith'.

This is an interesting concept, but many studies from Western society have shown that, on a person to person basis, the die-hard atheist is just as likely to undergo an NDE as the staunchest Christian believer (92).

There is a well known NDE account cited by Morse and Perry (83) from a 33 year old Muslim woman called Mebruke who was born in Saudi Arabia and was living in New York. She nearly drowned in a swimming accident in the Mediterranean Sea :-

'I was drifting in and out of consciousness during this time, and I could feel my spirit actually leaving my body. I saw and heard the conversations between my husband and the doctors taking place outside my room, about forty feet away down a hallway. I was later

able to verify this conversation to my shocked husband. Then I actually 'crossed over' to another dimension, where I was engulfed in a total feeling of love. I also experienced extreme clarity of why I had the cancer, why I had come into this life in the first place, what role everyone in my family played in my life in the grand scheme of things, and generally how life works. The clarity and understanding I obtained in this state is almost indescribable. Words seem to limit the experience—I was at a place where I understood how much more there is than what we are able to conceive in our 3-dimensional world. I realized what a gift life was, and that I was surrounded by loving spiritual beings, who were always around me even when I did not know it. '

This NDE, with its autoscopic component, its enhanced clarity of thought and its proximity to beings of unbounded love is very much the Western type of experience. Since Mebruke was living in New York, had the influence of her Islamic cultural heritage been, at least to some degree, negated by Westernised living ?

3. Buddhism

Buddhism originated in India between the 6th and 4th centuries BC, from where it spread through much of Asia. Today there are about 500 million followers worldwide. The founder, Gautama Buddha, was born into a wealthy, princely family, but shunned this existence to live a simple contemplative life in the quest to end suffering and thus achieve true happiness. Buddhism embraces the Hindu doctrines of reincarnation and karma, as well as striving for the ultimate goal of escaping the cycle of death and rebirth. However, in contrast to

Hinduism, Buddhists do not believe that the soul is eternal, but rather the human 'self' comprises a spurious assortment of habits, memories, sensations and desires which can be reincarnated in body after body. Since life in the corporeal body is viewed negatively as the source of suffering, Buddhists strive to achieve release or liberation (Nirvana) by dismantling and jettisoning the false sense of 'self'. In this way, nothing is left to reincarnate and hence there is nothing to experience pain.

There exists a remarkable Buddhist text, the Bardo Thodol, commonly known in the West as 'The Tibetan Book of the Dead', which is believed to have been composed in the 8th century AD by the legendary Padma Sambhava. The text is, in essence, an instructive guide outlining the journey of the soul which takes place in the interval between death and the next rebirth (the Bardo). The tracts are read aloud to those at the point of death in order for them to understand the nature of their consciousness and thus attain liberation from the cycle of rebirth. In this way, the dead are able to recognise paths to the heavenly realms and achieve Nirvana, rather than entering into the lower planes, where reincarnation continues.

What is remarkable is the fact that the description of life after death contained in the Bardo Thodol shows strong parallels with the classic NDE. The Tibetan text relates that the mind or soul leaves the body and finds itself in a void. Alarming or disturbing noises may be heard before the soul becomes aware that it resides outside of the physical body it once inhabited. Distraught relatives can be seen praying near to the body. Communication with the mourners is attempted, but frustratingly nobody seems to respond. The dead person then realises he still has a body, but this 'shining' body is without material substance. He can pass through solid objects without hindrance and travel is almost instantaneous, achieved simply by the power of thought. His mind becomes very lucid and his senses keener. If, in life, he suffered any disability to his mortal body, he finds his 'shining' body to be free from all such ailments and impediments. He may encounter other beings in the same state as him and see a clear, pure light. Serene feelings of contentment overwhelm him. In a mirror he sees all the worthy and dishonourable actions he carried out in life, made manifest to both himself and the beings judging him to see vividly.

A classic Buddhist NDE is described in the biography of the 16th century delok (one who has returned from death), Lingza Chokyi. She had 'died' and found herself outside her body. She frantically tried to communicate with her family as they set about preparing for the funeral. Frustration turned to anger as they took no notice of her. However these negative feelings dissipated into immeasurable happiness when she finally came before 'the master' and their minds melded. She heard what she took to be her father calling her and she followed the voice to meet the Lord of Death who was assessing the good and evil actions of the dead. At this place she encountered the souls of others who recounted their stories. Suddenly Lingza was sent back to her earthly body as there had been an error concerning her name and family and it was not yet her time to die (*93*).

This narrative contains elements from both the Bardo Thedol and experiences described by Western near-death survivors.

It is interesting to note that the Asian concept of an error having been made, through selecting the wrong person to be brought into the afterlife, is present in this account from some 500 years ago.

There are a number of recent NDE reports from those of the Buddhist faith in Thailand. In nearly all cases, the first event to be described is seeing two or more strangers, usually identified as Yamatoots (messengers of the Lord of the Dead, Yama). They take the person's spirit away, quite often forcibly and against their will, to be judged by Yama. Some examples are given below (*94*) :-

'You're coming with us', or *'we've come to take you to Hell'* or *'it is your turn to die'* are phrases commonly reported. Often the Yamatoots show the new arrival a dreadful place which he/she identifies as Hell .

'A grey mist covered everything. Then I saw a crowd of skeletons. I knew where I was. I was in a different world. I was in hell', and

'we came to another torture area. I saw a path of hot coals. The guard was forcing people to walk this path...the Yamatoot explained this path was for those who had too many defilements', and

'I could hear the cries of those being tortured'.

The Yamahoots then show the newcomer a heavenly place.

' I was then transported to Heaven. I felt happy because it was quiet and the air was cool, fresh and smelled of flowers. I saw yellow flowers with a beautiful fragrance. The Yamahoot took me up 27 levels. I saw many beautiful things in Heaven. There were lovely pavilions, where jewellery littered the ground', and,

'I saw a garden with trees all in rows. It was very beautiful, like a garden of a king or millionaire. As I walked into the garden, I smelled some flowers. They were so very fragrant, with a scent i had never known before. Next, I saw some angels, both male and female. They glided

through the air. They were dressed beautifully and wore exquisite jewellery'.

The meeting with Yama then usually follows. Yama is often condemnatory in his judgement.

'Yama said that I had committed many sins and sentenced me to many rebirths both as a chicken and many other kinds of bird....he commanded a Yamahoot to take me to a place where I was to receive additional punishments', and,

Yama told me that I had committed many sins, especially in having butchered a number of chickens.

A significant number of these Buddhist NDEs again cite the reason for return as having been wrongly indentified by the Yamahoots.

In most cases, those having undergone an NDE feel that they have been shown the path to Nirvana and the way to live better lives.

There are many contrasts between these Thai Buddhist NDEs and those from Western society. Seeing a bright light and travelling along a tunnel to reach it, absent in the former are common in the latter. Nearly all Thai NDEs feature a vision of Hell, whereas in the West, horrific NDEs are far less common, though it must be stressed that in no case did a Thai soul experience torture directed at themselves. In Thai NDEs dead friends and relatives occasionally appear, not to greet and welcome the soul, but simply to inform the newly-arrived spirit of afterlife protocol in a matter-of-fact manner (95).

For those of either Hindu or Buddhist faiths, the bright shining light of the Being of total love and understanding is replaced by Yamraj or

Yama, who is far removed from the compassionate entity seen by those in the West. More often than not, Yama appears as a wrathful being and is remembered for his power to condemn one to Hell.

The manner of entry into the afterlife in Asian NDEs is often described in terms of 'walking', 'running' or being 'taken by others', rather than an automatic 'floating away' from your corpse below. A commonly reported feature with Buddhists regarding return to their body involves falling or tripping over an object and regaining consciousness when their spirit hits the ground. I am unaware of any Western NDE that reports such an event.

As regards to other religions, such as Judaism, Guru Nanak and the Sikh tradition and the Chinese faiths of Confucianism and Taoism, there are occasional NDE reports, but too few to draw any firm conclusions regarding the effect of culture on events occurring in afterlife visions.

From the accounts given above,, it does appear that cultural traditions, etched deep in the psyche do affect the course of events which take place after death. In many Western NDEs, the person chooses to return after being given the option to stay or not. Perhaps this reflects the high degree of freedom and independence Westerners enjoy in comparison to those of Thai or Indian cultures, where dependence on one's family, tradition and religion are encouraged. The notion of having a choice about living or dying does not fit well in a culture where traditionally, one cannot choose one's spouse, work, religion, or where to live.

The vast majority of Thai NDEs feature a strong and vivid account of both Heaven and Hell, together with the principal event of being subjected to judgement. This perception is far less pronounced in

Western NDEs, where religious beliefs, if they exist at all, are usually looser and less dogmatic. Interestingly Atwater (96) found that NDE reports from the so called 'Bible Belt' in south-eastern USA, where the bible scriptures are taken literally, are more likely to contain mention of Hell and associated horrors.

Thus, it appears that the mechanism for the potential generation of the NDE is present in all human brains, but that the interpretation of events within the experience is strongly influenced by cultural upbringing.

CHAPTER 9

PSYCHOMETRIC SCALES TO MEASURE NDEs
(Facts and Figures)

It was not long after research into NDE's began in earnest that the need to positively identify and quantify the phenomenon became apparent. Taken in isolation, feelings of bliss, travelling through a tunnel, seeing bright lights and the impression of floating outside the body can be experienced when the brain is not *in extremis.* What was needed for an event to be classified as an NDE was the identification of a series of common features which all researchers could follow.

Thus, in 1980, Ring devised the 'weighted core experience index', often referred to as the WCEI (*97*). He identified ten NDE features from his own research and from the findings of others. Each component was ascribed different weights to give a maximum score of 29. A score greater than 6 was considered to represent a true NDE event. Data retrieved from the accounts of near-death survivors were now made quantifiable. Ring's criteria are :-

1. Subjective sense of being dead.

2. Feelings of peace, painlessness etc.

3. Sense of separation from the body.

4. Sense of entering a dark region or tunnel.

5. Entering or encountering a presence / hearing a voice.

6. Taking stock of one's life.

7. Seeing or being enveloped by light.

8. Seeing beautiful colours.

9. Entering into the light.

10. Encountering visible spirits.

In 1983, the American psychiatrist Bruce Greyson modified and expanded the WCEI with his final version listing 16 features which are divided into 4 groups ; cognitive, affective, paranormal and transcendental.

The scale has a maximum score of 32, with a score of 7 or higher being the criterion for a true NDE (*98*).

 Greyson's scale is now widely used by researchers and has been shown to have good test - retest reliability and internal consistency.

The questions asked of patients, with 'depth' scores are given below. As an example of the results obtained in one such study, Greyson's percentages of individuals who identified the various features as being peculiar to their own NDE are also included. The total number of respondents was 183, where 69 (38%) were male and 114 (62%) were female, with a mean age of 32.5 years (*99*).

Cognitive component

1. **_Did time seem to speed up or slow down ?_**

0 = No, 1= Time seemed to go faster or slower than usual, 2= Everything seemed to be happening at once, or time stopped or lost all meaning.

No= 16%, 1=10%, 2= 74%

2. **_Were your thoughts speeded up ?_**

0= No, 1=Faster than usual, 2= Incredibly fast

No= 58%, 1=16%, 2=26%

3. **_Did scenes from your past come back to you ?_**

0= No, 1= I remembered past events, 2= My past flashed before me.

0=75%, 1=8%, 2=17%

4. **_Did you suddenly seem to understand everything ?_**

0= No, 1= Everything about myself or others, 2= Everything about the universe.

0=46%, 1=19%, 2=35%

Affective component

1. **_Did you have a feeling of peace or pleasantness ?_**

0= No, 1= Relief or calmness, 2= Incredible peace or pleasantness.

0=8%, 1=18%, 2=74%

2. **_Did you have a feeling of joy ?_**

0= No, 1= Happiness, 2= Incredible joy.

1=23%, 1=20%, 2=57%

3. *Did you feel a sense of harmony or unity with the universe ?*

0= No, 1= I felt no longer in conflict with nature, 2= I felt one with the world.

0=22%, 1=23%, 2=55%

4.*Did you see or feel surrounded by a brilliant light ?*

0= No, 1= An unusually bright light, 2= A light clearly of mystical or other worldly origin.

0=28%, 1=26%, 2=46%

Paranormal component

1. *Were your senses more vivid than usual ?*

0= No, 1= More vivid than usual, 2= Incredibly more vivid.

0=34%, 1=26%, 2=40%

2. *Did you seem to be aware of things going on elsewhere, as if by extrasensory perception ?*

0= No, 1= Yes, but the facts have not been checked out, 2= Yes, and the facts have been corroborated.

0=66%, 1=20%, 2= 14%

3. *Did scenes from the future come to you ?*

0= No, 1= Scenes from my personal future, 2= Scenes from the world's future.

0=80%, 1= 9%, 2= 11%

4. *Did you feel separated from your body ?*

0=No, 1= I lost awareness of my body, 2= I clearly left my body and existed outside it.

0=14%, 1= 31%, 2= 55%

Transcendental component

1. *Did you seem to enter some other unearthly world ?*

0= No, 1= Some unfamiliar and strange place, 2= A clearly mystical or unearthly realm.

0=24%, 1= 20%, 2= 56%

2. *Did you seem to encounter a mystical being or hear an unidentifiable voice ?*

0= No, 1= I heard a voice I could not identify, 2= I encountered a definite being or a voice clearly of mystical or unearthly origin.

0= 41%, 1=9%, 2=50%

3. *Did you see deceased or religious spirits ?*

0= No, 1= I sensed their presence, 2= I actually saw them.

0=64%, 1=11%, 2=25%

4. *Did you come to a border or a point of no return ?*

0= No, 1= I came to a definite conscious decision to return to life, 2= I came to a barrier that I was not permitted to cross or was sent back against my will.

0=31%, 1=30%, 2=39%

A total score of 7 or higher is considered an NDE for research purposes. The mean score among a large data sample is 15. As far as individual component features are concerned, a cognitive event is assigned to a score of 5 or higher. A transcendental experience is assigned to a cognitive score of less than 5 and transcendental score of 5 or higher. An affective event is identified by cognitive and transcendental scores are both less than 5 with the affective score of 5 or more. A paranormal experience is ascribed when all of the other three components score less than 5, with a paranormal score of 5 or greater.

The results from the study cited above show about one third of the experiences met the criteria for Cognitive NDEs, and a quarter each identified as Affective and Transcendental NDEs. Very few could be classified as Paranormal and 18% of experiences could not be classified within the framework laid down.

When both 1 and 2 depth scale responses are combined, the eight most prevalent features of the NDE were, in order :-

1. Feeling of peace, 92%

2. Sense of leaving your body, 86%

3. Sense of a change in the rate of the passage of time, 84%

4. Feeling at one with nature / the universe, 78%

5. Feeling of happiness / joy, 77%

6. Visiting an unfamiliar or mystical place, 76%

7. Seeing a bright light, 72%.

8. Sensing a barrier / being sent back / deciding to return, 69%.

In this survey, the number of responses describing encounters with deceased relatives or with a mystical being did not feature highly. It may be that the Transcendental experiences occur later in the progression of an NDE and that some patients were successfully resuscitated before they reached the later stages.

There is an interesting disparity between research data regarding the frequency of NDEs reported by those who suffered life-threatening illness. Morse saw 85% amongst children (100), Ring recorded 48% experiencing an NDE from a population with a mean age of 37 years (97) and Sabom 43% amongst a group with mean age of 49 (101). These findings contrast with Van Lommel's study in which only 18% of patients reported a NDE. Here the mean patient age was 62 years (76).

These results would suggest that the younger the patient, the greater the chance of experiencing a NDE. However, this can be offset, to some degree, by the fact that a person of say 30 years has a better chance of survival than someone double that age (especially in coronary crisis) and hence is more likely to 'return' and relate their story.

Why a substantial number of 'critical condition' patients report no NDE in their unconscious state has yet to be determined. Reluctance to tell others of their experience or loss of memory of the event seem inadequate explanations.

CHAPTER 10

THE 'AWARE' RESEARCH STUDY

The study of death has traditionally been the preserve of theologians and philosophers. However, such is the recent interest in the near-death-experience among physicians and psychologists, that a large, multidisciplinary research programme has been instigated, involving more than 25 major medical centres throughout Europe, Canada and the United States. This enterprise, the AWARE (AWAreness during REsusciation) study began in 2008, and is led by Dr. Sam Parnia, a renowned authority on human consciousness, together with Dr. Peter Fenwick and Professors Stephen Holgate and Robert Peveler of the University of Southampton.

Anecdotal evidence, of which there is a multitude in the field of near-death-experiences, does not sit well with the rigour of scientific analysis. Thus, the AWARE study uses the latest technologies to examine the brain and consciousness during cardiac arrest. Cardiac arrest was chosen for specific study since all three criteria of death are present ; the heart stops beating, the lungs become inoperative and the brain ceases to function. Dr. Parnia explains the scope of the AWARE research in this way :-

'The remarkable point about these experiences, (NDEs) is that while studies of the brain during cardiac arrest have consistently shown that there is no measurable brain activity, these subjects have reported detailed perceptions that indicate the contrary—namely, a high level of consciousness in the absence of detectable brain activity. If we can objectively verify these claims, the results would bear profound implications not only for the scientific community, but for the way in which we understand and relate to life and death as a society.'

An interesting feature included in the AWARE study is testing the validity of out-of-body experiences by deploying randomly generated, hidden images in positions that are not visible unless viewed from specific elevated vantage points. For example near the ceilings of resuscitation suites and the like.

Preliminary findings were published in December, 2014 (*102*). A synopsis of the data obtained is as follows:-

1. Of 2060 patients in this study, only 140 survived and were well enough to undergo a preliminary interview. Of these, 39 were not able to complete a second interview, mostly due to fatigue.

2. Of the remaining 101 patients, information from a second interview showed only 9 (9%) were deemed to have had an NDE.

3. Of these 9 patients, only 2 reported memories of auditory/visual awareness of the physical environment.

4. Of these 2, one was not able to follow up with an in depth third interview, due to ill health.

5. The one remaining NDEer had verifiable recollections of events following his cardiac arrest.

 This patient felt euphoric and heard an automated voice saying 'shock the patient, shock the patient'. The patient rose to the ceiling and looked down on his physical body and saw a nurse and another man who was 'chunky' and bald. The next day the patient recognised the bald man who attended the resuscitation. The medical record confirmed the use of an Automated External Defibrillator that would give the automated instructions that the patient heard.

6. Tantalisingly, both cases of cardiac arrest, in which awareness of the physical environment occurred, took place in non-acute areas of the hospital, where there no hidden images were lodged.

On the face of it, the results are disappointing. The AWARE study, given its wide geographical scope, provided real potential for proving, once and for all, the existence of consciousness outside of the non-functioning brain. All that has been achieved out of the analysis of 2060 cardiac arrest patients over four years is just one individual who has had an 'interesting' and verifiable OBE, but one that falls short of many more descriptive and persuasive documented examples cited elsewhere in the literature. There was not a single case where hidden images were identified

Firstly, the problem boils down to numbers. Only a fraction of those suffering cardiac arrest survived and a significant proportion of these people were too unwell to give a meaningful interview. Ideally, we should be looking at around 10,000 subjects in the first instance.

Secondly, the placement sites of target images needs to be reassessed. The assumption that OBEers float up close to the ceiling and are looking downwards comes from many reports. However, where exactly near the ceiling are they ? At what angle and perspective are they looking down at their body ? An image on top of a shelf or cupboard might well be out of their line of sight. Also, the focus of interest for the disembodied spirit seems to come from intense fascination and concentration on the frantic revival efforts below, rather than casually looking round at the decor. One more thing to note is not all OBEers report being in an elevated position. Some simply mention walking around the room, peering over the doctor's shoulder and trying unsuccessfully to communicate with the resuscitation team.

Perhaps filling every available space with a particularly eye-catching image that can only be seen from above head height might be a way forward.

Thirdly, less than half the patients were treated for cardiac arrest in areas with hidden images. Thus even if someone reported an NDE with component OBE, their chances of seeing the image would have been extremely low.

In 2016, the AWARE study II got underway, with a change in design strategy. In this second project, Emergency Department or Research staff will be alerted to cases of cardiac arrest and will attend with portable brain oxygen monitoring devices and a tablet which will display visual images upwards above the patient as resuscitation is taking place. Measurements obtained during cardiac arrest will be used to compare data from all cardiac arrest patients independent of outcome [whether they live or die]. Survivors will then be followed up and with their consent have in-depth, audio recorded interviews.

In this way, with distinctive images being placed in close proximity to the patient, but not in their visual field, it is hoped to maximize the possibility of obtaining the crucial data the study seeks.

CHAPTER 11

LOOKING FOR EXPLANATIONS

The near-death experience is an event which transcends national boundaries and its manifestation can be traced throughout recorded history. The power and sophistication of modern medicine has allowed the return of thousands of people who would have previously been bound for the grave, never to tell their tale. As a consequence, there has been a surge in the number of NDE accounts from survivors over the last 40 years or so. This has provided a rich source of new information for psychologists and neurophysiologists to pore over and has sparked fierce debate as to the precise nature of the phenomenon. As most religious faiths speak of an afterlife, many regard the NDE as clear confirmation of their beliefs. Others are much more sceptical and view the whole experience as being the product of an aberration of brain function.

1. <u>NEUROPHYSIOLOGICAL CHANGES FOLLOWING CARDIAC ARREST</u>

Before we look at specific areas of research in brain chemistry related to NDEs, let's deal with established medical facts about what happens to the body when the heart ceases to beat.

Brain function is known to be severely compromised following cardiac arrest. A state of unconsciousness rapidly develops, together with the abolition of all body reflexes through loss of brain stem activity, for example, pupils become fixed and dilated. The respiratory centre close to the brain stem also fails and breathing stops. An anoxic internal environment then develops to which the brain is particularly sensitive. Electrical activity in both the cerebral cortex and the deeper structures of the brain is known to cease after a very short period of time and progression to a state of complete isoelectricity always occurs within 20 seconds (103). Cardiac electrical shock, administered by the use of a defibrillator, can restore normal blood pressure within seconds if heart stimulation is successful, but restoration of normal electroencephalogram activity may not return for many minutes, or even hours (104)

When the resuscitation records of patients who have undergone an NDE are checked, their medical circumstances dictate that there must have been a total lack of electrical activity, in both the cortex and the brain-stem. How then are they able to recall clear, detailed accounts ? As Van Lommel (105) puts it :-

'Such a brain (one displaying no electrical activity) would be roughly analogous to a computer with its power source unplugged and its circuits detached. It could not hallucinate ; it could do nothing at all.....the paradoxical occurrence of heightened, lucid awareness and thought processes during a period of impaired cerebral perfusion during cardiac arrest raises particular perplexing questions for our current understanding of consciousness and its relation to brain function.

The neurophysiological account above leads us on to research work that has been undertaken into chemical and psychological aspects of the NDE phenomenon.

2. <u>RECREATIONAL DRUGS</u>

Early scientific attention focused on drug involvement in the precipitation of the NDE. It has been well known for many years that anaesthetic gases such as nitrous oxide can produce mystical experiences as can recreational use of psychedelic compounds such as LSD (lysergic acid diethylamide) and DMT (dimethyltryptamine). Some researchers believe that a rapid release of DMT from the pineal gland in a brain under stress leads to the NDE (106). There are two problems here. Firstly, only a tiny proportion of patients that have been studied were under the influence of any hallucinatory drug at the time of their experience. The only drug which may be given to say a cardiac arrest patient is adrenaline, which has no effect on brain function *per se.* Secondly, mind-expanding substances give very different experiences from person to person. Ten people taking an identical dose of LSD or DMT might all report the morphing of objects, intensification of colours and heightened spiritual awareness, but the context of their experience would be diverse, quite unlike those who have undergone a NDE.

The anaesthetic drug ketamine is widely used as a pain reliever in both animals and humans. It is the doctors' drug of choice for people in traumatic shock who are at risk of hypotension, but is also used recreationally. Ketamine can induce experiences similar to the NDE such as leaving the body, accompanied by a feeling of peace and tranquility. Ketamine is thought to block receptors which bind to glutamate which is an excitatory chemical messenger in the human brain. Jansen (107) has proposed that the production of endogenous ketamine-like chemicals in the brain of a dying person can account for an NDE. However, ketamine-induced experiences are usually random and bizarre and users appreciate the illusory nature of their experience.

Contrast this to the convincing reality of true NDEs, such as those described in earlier chapters.

3. <u>BLOOD GASES</u>

Oxygen starvation was another early causative candidate for study. Certainly, lack of oxygen might well be expected in those patients with no detectable heartbeat and/or very low blood pressure. Indeed, normal brain functioning is critically dependent on a rich supply of oxygen. The British psychologist Dr Susan Blackmore believes that lack of oxygen is the trigger for the tunnel event in the NDE. Anoxic conditions in the visual cortex of the brain cause disinhibition of the neurons which start to fire randomly, producing 'neural noise'. Because far more nerve cells are devoted to the centre of the visual field than its periphery, more random firing will occur at the centre of the field than at the edge. Hence the appearance of an image having a bright core, with a darkened surround, giving the impression of a tunnel with a light at the end of it (*108*). This theory is supported, to some degree, by reports from high-speed jet fighter pilots who are subject to very high G forces, especially when making rapid changes in flight direction. Such manoeuvres can result in a sudden reduction in the flow of blood to the brain, potentially leading to unconsciousness and fatal consequences. Under these conditions, pilots have reported tunnel vision and dreamlike states, as well as feelings of detachment and euphoria (109)

Another region of the brain which has come under scrutiny is the temporal lobe, which is associated with emotion and memory and is particularly sensitive to lack of oxygen. Could anoxia trigger the strong personal feelings characteristic of the NDE ? Well maybe, but memory would also be severely impaired, which is the antithesis of the clear, vivid recollections of near-death survivors.

The effects of oxygen starvation on healthy subjects are well known. Mental confusion and impaired cognitive ability precede unconsciousness. Those who have been accidentally deprived of oxygen or deliberately so, for example in laboratory studies, do not report features of the NDE when they regain consciousness. Also there are many documented instances where vivid NDEs have occurred when blood oxygen levels have been normal.

Concomitant with lowering levels of oxygen in the body during heart stoppage or cessation of breathing is the rise of carbon dioxide concentration which is produced by the respiring tissues. As with oxygen deprivation, the effects of hypercarbia on the brain have been well documented. In a controlled study aimed at proving that hypercarbia would be effective in the treatment of patients with certain psychiatric disorders, American psychiatrist Dr L. Meduna, gave his subjects a mixture of 70% oxygen and 30% carbon dioxide to breathe. These gas concentrations were around 2.5 and 1000 times more concentrated than in 'normal air' respectively. Interestingly, Meduna's patients reported a number of experiences which are closely akin to the NDE, such as :-

'I was looking down on myself, as though I was way out here in space'

And :-

'I felt myself being separated; my soul drawing apart from the physical being and was drawn upward seemingly to leave the earth and to go upward, where it reached a greater spirit with whom there was a

communion, producing a remarkable, new relaxation and deep security'. (*110*)

These findings would appear to constitute compelling evidence for the involvement of high carbon dioxide levels in the brain as the mechanism for NDE generation, especially as Meduna's subjects were reporting similar experiences. There are some problems however. Hypercarbia also produces images more associated with mind-expanding drugs, such as the personification of inanimate objects which are not reported in NDEs. Hypercarbia-induced muscle spasms are also absent in NDEers. Note also that Maduna's subjects were given an excess of oxygen in their breathing mixture. Their brains were never starved of oxygen. In say a patient suffering cardiac arrest, while carbon dioxide levels rise, oxygen levels fall substantially. As we have seen, the anoxic neural environment is hardly conducive for the development of the clear, lucid recall of the near-death returnees. Indeed, the brain is even more sensitive to oxygen starvation than to an excess of carbon dioxde. Also, there are many recorded instances where NDEs have occurred when carbon dioxide levels have been found to be normal. Therefore, although hypercarbia remains a candidate for involvement in the NDE, in isolation it by no means provides an explanation for the total phenomenon.

4. <u>THE DEPERSONALISATION MODEL</u>

Another way of explaining the out-of-body experience is through 'depersonalisation', as described by Noyes and Kletti (*111*). This term describes a psychological defence against the threat of death when an individual <u>perceives</u> imminent danger. The mind replaces the real world with pleasing fantasies. A good example has been reported by

Moody (*112*), where a man was involved in a motor vehicle accident, but sustained only very light injuries and was never physically close to death :-

'I lost control of my car on a curve and the car left the road and went in the air and I remember seeing the blue sky and saw that the car was going down into a ditch. At the time the car left the road, I said to myself, 'I'm in an accident'. At that point, I kind of lost my sense of time and I lost my reality as far as my body is concerned - I lost touch with my body. My being, or my 'self', or my spirit, whatever you would like to label it-- I could sort of feel it rise out of me, out through my head. and it wasn't anything that hurt, it was just sort of like a lifting and it being above me... My being felt like it had a density to it...it was small and felt like it was sort of circular, with no rigid outline to it. You could liken it to a cloud...as if it was in its own encasement. As it went out of my body, it seemed that the large end left first and the small end last. When my being was suspended above my head, it was almost like it was trying to decide whether it wanted to leave or stay. It seemed then as though time was standing still'.

Endorphins are suspected to play a role in depersonalisation (*113*) The word endorphin literally means 'morphine produced inside the body'. These endogenous opioid neuropeptides are produced by the central nervous system and the pituitary gland, their primary function being to inhibit the transmission of pain signals. They may also elicit a feeling of high-wellbeing and detachment from the body (*114*). Thus pain, or even the thought of experiencing pain can stimulate their production in the body.

Although cases such as that related above are of interest and may represent a component of the NDE phenomenon, they do not explain the cognitive memory of near-death events gathered by the deeply unconscious brain. Strong spiritual feelings, often a feature of the aftermath of a true near-death event, are also absent.

5. <u>THE DYING BRAIN HYPOTHESIS</u>

In her book, 'Dying to Live' (108), Susan Blackmore disparages any notion of the transcendental interpretation of the NDE. She ascribes the consistent features of NDE reports from those near death to the fact that we all have similar neural connections and brain chemistry. As discussed earlier, she attributes the 'tunnel and the light' to a direct consequence of anoxia. The 'life review', she says, can be explained by temporal lobe seizures triggered by endorphin production and the 'out-of-body' experience can be attributed to the breakdown of body image and model of reality during extreme mental anguish. These explanations are plausible and may well play a part in the overall NDE event. However, she is on much more shaky ground when attempting to explain the many instances of accurate perception and recall of events which took place in the immediate environment of deeply unconscious people. What would be her explanation for this account by Dutch physician Pim Van Lommel who received a patient with a very poor prognosis under his care?

'During the night shift, an ambulance brings in a 44-year-old cyanotic, comatose man into the coronary care unit...When we want to intubate the patient he turns out to have dentures in his mouth. I remove these dentures and put them in the 'crash car'. Meanwhile we continue extensive CPR. After about an hour and a half the patient has sufficient

heart rhythm and blood pressure, but he is still ventilated and intubated and he is still comatose...after a week I meet again with the patient...the moment he sees me he says ' Oh, that nurse knows where my dentures are'. I am very surprised. Then he elucidates, 'Yes, you were there when I was brought into hospital...and you took my dentures out of my mouth and put them into that 'car', it had all these bottles on it and there was the sliding drawer underneath where you put my teeth'. I was especially amazed because I remember this happening when the man was in deep coma and in the process of CPR. When I asked further, it appeared the man had seen himself lying in bed, that he had perceived how the nurses and doctors had been busy with CPR. He was able to describe correctly and in detail the small room in which he was resuscitated as well as the appearance of those present like myself...he is deeply impressed with his experience and says he is no longer afraid of death...4 weeks later he left hospital as a healthy man'. (105).

The Blackmore model, in explaining the above account, would suggest that fantasy, prior knowledge, lucky guessing, together with the residual operating senses of hearing and touch were involved in the reconstruction of the NDE event in the mind of the patient.

5. **BIRTH MEMORIES**

Some researchers have likened the NDE with the birth event experienced by the neonate and suggest that at death, the mind recapitulates this occurrence (115). This hypothesis has also been put forward by Carl Sagan in his book 'Broca's brain' (116). The model has become known as the 'near-birth experience'. Parallels include the trauma of being forced to leave a warm, safe, familiar environment. The movement along the birth canal being representative of travel inside a tunnel, with the final emergence into light at the end of that tunnel. These analogies are intriguing, but it is difficult to understand how a new-born child could perceive and retain memory of such events, given the immaturity of neural connections in the brain at such a young age (117). Also, almost invariably, infants' eyes are closed at the point of birth. Further doubt about the validity of this model comes from studies which show that those born by Caesarean section are just as likely to encounter an NDE as those born vaginally (118).

CHAPTER 12

NDES AND THE NATURE OF CONSCIOUSNESS

The perplexing and paradoxical nature of NDEs has led to deeper questions being asked as to the nature of consciousness.

The dictionary definition of consciousness is :- the awareness of external events, internal sensations, the self and thoughts about experiences. Certainly the brain with its 90 billion neurones and incredibly complex synaptic interconnections is the receiver and processor of external and internal stimuli and there is little doubt that thought is a function of the brain

The crucial question is whether consciousness is separate (or can be separated) from the brain and survive the inevitable destruction of the body at death. If this is not the case, then the belief in reincarnation or any form of afterlife is severely undermined. Thus two basic theories exist. Firstly the 'productive' theory would argue that NDEs are last gasp manifestations conjured by the dying brain and that consciousness is extinguished at death. Secondly, the 'transmissive' theory admits probable correlations with brain processes, but leaves open the possibility that death is not an annihilation but a transformation of consciousness (119). Interestingly, OBEs do not necessarily occur when a person is near death, but they are recognised as one of the more common features of the NDE. Perhaps this can be taken as evidence that a person's consciousness can indeed detach itself temporarily from the brain during life and then permanently at the point of death. The separated consciousness views its former harbour in the body below without emotion, as from an old coat which has been discarded....the butterfly from its chrysalis.

More recently, interest has turned to quantum physics to provide an explanation for aspects of consciousness during cardiac arrest. This complex scientific discipline may provide help in understanding the transition between the fields of consciousness in the phase-space (a multidimensional space containing all possible states of a system) and the body-linked waking consciousness in the real space (space in the real world). It is these two complimentary aspects of consciousness (120) that are of interest. This hypothesis suggests that the human consciousness originates from and is stored in the phase-space and the brain only serves as a relay station. A comparison can be made with the Internet, which does not originate from the computer itself, but is only received by it. Van Lommel (105) makes the pertinent observation :-

'In trying to understand this concept of quantum mechanical mutual interaction between the invisible phase-space and our visible, material body, it seems appropriate to compare it with modern worldwide communication. There is a continuous exchange of objective information by means of electromagnetic fields for radio, TV, mobile telephone, or laptop computer. We are not consciously aware of the vast amounts of electromagnetic fields that constantly, day and night, exist around us and are even permeating us, as well as permeating structures like walls and buildings, also at this very moment. We only become aware of these electromagnetic informative fields at the moment we use our mobile telephone or by switching on our radio, TV,

or laptop. What we receive is neither inside the instrument, nor in the components, but thanks to the receiver, the information from the electromagnetic fields becomes observable to our senses and hence perception occurs in our consciousness. The voice we hear over our telephone is not inside the telephone. The concert we hear over our radio is transmitted to our radio. The images and music we hear and see on TV are transmitted to our TV set. We can receive what is transmitted with the speed of light from a distance of some hundreds or thousands of miles. And if we switch off the TV set, the reception disappears, but the transmission continues. The information transmitted remains present within the electromagnetic fields. The connection has been interrupted, but it is not vanished and still can be received elsewhere by using another TV set ("non-locality").'

Thus, the quantum model allows us to understand, not only that consciousness can be experienced independently of brain function, but also will continue to exist after bodily demise. The invisible, immaterial phase-space dimension becomes its harbour, in which all past, present and future is enclosed.

For those of faith, here is the scientific evidence to support what they already knew. Everyone has an immortal soul which leaves the body at death and transcends to another realm.....the teaching of all the world's major religions.

For the sceptic , the application of quantum physics and quantum mechanics is the last desperate attempt by proponents of life-after-death to conjure up some rarified mathematical model in order to further their belief. For example, fellow Dutch physician G.M. Woerlee has stated that Van Lommel's thoughts on quantum consciousness are

full of 'tendentious and suggestive pseudoscientific nonsense.'(121).
Others have taken a much less acerbic view and regard it as an
interesting line of enquiry which merits further investigation.

In summary, the near-death-experience is an intriguing subject because
proving its existence over and above simple aberrations of a dying brain
has profound implications in the worlds of theology, science and
medicine.
As we have seen, the crucial question is whether consciousness can
survive outside of the brain. If it can, we can all consider ourselves, not
only immortal , but also having the potential for reincarnation.

 The battle between the sceptics and believers continues to rage.

One day we will all have a chance to find out the truth when our time
comes, but as my old R.E. school teacher once said to our class :-

*'If there is an afterlife, believers will feel vindicated and sceptics proved
wrong. If there isn't, sceptics can't feel vindicated and believers remain
oblivious to their misconception'.*

APPENDIX

A Profile of Leading Research Workers in the Field of Near-Death Studies.

Dr. P.M.H. Atwater, born 1937 in Idaho, USA, is one of the original researchers in the field of near-death studies, having begun her work in 1978. Specialising in the NDE, the after effects of spiritual experiences and the transformation of consciousness, she herself is a near-death survivor, having undergone three separate events in 1977.

Dr. Susan Blackmore, born 1951, is a British parapsychologist, lecturer and freelance writer. Despite, personally, having experienced an out-of-body episode whilst studying at Oxford University, she is well known for her sceptical stance on any paranormal involvement in near-death-experiences. From the research she has carried out she claims no psychic phenomena were found - only wishful thinking, self-deception, experimental error and occasionally fraud. She is a Fellow of the Committee for Sceptical Enquiry.

Chris Carter, born in Canada, he received his undergraduate and Master's degrees from Oxford University. Holding completely divergent views to Blackmore, he is a vocal critic of Materialism and the view that everything we experience can be reduced to just brain activity.

Dr. Peter Fenwick, born 1935, is a British neurophysiologist and Cambridge University graduate, with consultancies at a number of UK hospitals. From his collection and analysis of over 300 NDEs, Fenwick argues that human consciousness can survive bodily death and is more than just a function of the brain.

Prof. Chris French, born 1956 is a British psychologist specialising in paranormal beliefs and experiences. He is currently Professor of Psychology at Goldsmiths College, University of London. He frequently appears on Television and radio presenting a sceptical view on paranormal claims. To quote a recent comment of his, '*the more I learned about psychology the more I appreciated our potential for fooling ourselves. Although our cognitive systems are truly amazing, they are also subject to various cognitive biases that can lead us to misperceive, misremember and misinterpret situations in such a way that we might think we have experienced something paranormal when in fact we have not*'.

Prof. Bruce Greyson, born 1946, is Professor Emeritus of Psychiatry at the University of Virginia in Charlottesville. Greyson has been called the father of research into NDEs. His constructed scale to measure component aspects of NDEs has been widely used by other researchers in the field.

Elizabeth Kubler-Ross (1926-2004) was a Swiss-American psychiatrist. she was recognised as one of the leading authorities in the field of death, dying and transition. She made a special study of children and death.

Dr. Raymond Moody, born 1944, Georgia, USA is a philosopher, psychologist and physician. Renowned for his ground-breaking book

'Life after Life', published in 1975 and in which he first coined the phrase 'near-death-experience', (NDE). This work brought him wide public and scientific attention. Moody is a strong believer in the paranormal and asserts that NDEs are evidence for the afterlife, since they cannot be explained by neurochemistry.

Dr. Melvin Morse, born 1953 is an American medical doctor, specialising in Paediatric medicine at the University of Washington. Well known for his pioneering work on NDEs reported by children. His work has helped transcend NDE events from a 'fringe' area to one considered mainstream and medically valuable.

Dr. Sam Parnia is a British Assistant Professor of Medicine at the Stony Brook University School of Medicine, specialising in research into cardiopulmonary resuscitation. Parnia was the principal investigator of the AWARE study, launched in 2008. From his research and from that of others, Parnia has suggested that the mind is mediated by, but not produced by the brain, so giving veracity to the NDE.

Dr. Maurice Rawlings (1922-2010) was an American cardiologist, based in Chattanooga, Tennessee. The NDEs that he personally witnessed on hospital wards led him to make a significant contribution to the field. In particular, he was the first to note a significant number of 'hellish' or horrific experiences, which hitherto had been thought to be rare.

Prof. Kenneth Ring, born in San Francisco in 1936 is Professor Emeritus of Psychology at the University of Connecticut. He has conducted a wide range of research into the near-death phenomenon and is particularly noted for his work relating to NDEs described by those who were blind from birth. He believes in the possibility of reincarnation.

Dr. Michael Sabom, born 1954 is an American cardiologist and author, based in Atlanta, Georgia. He is a leading authority on near-death research, having gathered many accounts and conducted exhaustive studies from clinically dead patients who have described witnessing their own resuscitation from outside their body.

Pim Van Lommel, born 1943, is a Dutch author and researcher in the field of near-death studies. He studied medicine at Utrecht University, specialising in cardiology and worked as a cardiologist at the Rijnstate Hospital, Arnhem for 26 years. He is particularly noted for bringing concepts of quantum physics into play in order to explain the separation of consciousness from the brain.

Bibliography

1. Moody, R.A., *Life after Life,* Mockingbird *Books,* Covington, Georgia (Bantum edition), 1975, p 40-41.

2. Ibid, p36.

3. Sabom, M.B., *Recollections of Death,* Corgi Edition, 1982, p 116.

4. Ring, K., *Heading Towards Omega*, New York, Morrow, 1984, p 42.

5. Fenwick, P. and Fenwick, E. *The Truth in the Light,* BCA, 1995, p34-35.

6. Rawlings, M., *Beyond Death's Door,* Sheldon Press, 1979, p73-75

7. Sabom, M.B., *Recollections of Death,* Corgi Edition, 1982, p123-161.

8. Ring, K., *Life at Death. A scientific investigation of the Near-Death Experience,* Coward, Mc Cann and Geoghegan, 1980, p 51.

9. Sabom, M.B., *Recollections of Death,* Corgi Edition, 1982, p 55.

10. Ring, K., *Heading Towards Omega*, New York, Morrow, 1984 p 43.

11. Fenwick, P. and Fenwick, E. *The Truth in the Light,* BCA, 1995 p 27.

12. Gordon Thomas, *Issels: The Biography of a Doctor,* Hodder & Stoughton, 1975, p 161-2.

13. Clark Sharp, K. *The Journal of near-death studies,* Vol. 15, No. 3 1995.

14. Moody, R.A., *Life after Life,* Mockingbird *Books,* Covington, Georgia (Bantum edition), 1975, p 49.

15. Ibid. p 49-50.

16. Ibid. p 50

17. Ibid. p 45.

18. Ibid. p 44.

19. Myers, F.W.H, *Human Personality and its Survival of Bodily Death, 1903,* p 212- 217.

20. Moody, R.A., *Life after Life,* Mockingbird *Books,* Covington, Georgia (Bantum edition), 1975, p 46.

21. Ibid, p 32.

22. Fenwick, P. and Fenwick, E. *The Truth in the Light,* BCA, 1995, p 53.

23. Moody, R.A., *Life after Life,* Mockingbird *Books,* Covington, Georgia (Bantum edition), 1975, p 33.

24. Fenwick, P. and Fenwick, E. *The Truth in the Light,* BCA, 1995, p 51.

25. Rawlings, M., *Beyond Death's Door,* Sheldon Press, 1979, p 80-81.

26. Sabom, M.B., *Recollections of Death,* Corgi Edition, 1982, p 64.

27. Fenwick, P. and Fenwick, E. *The Truth in the Light,* BCA, 1995, p 31.

28. Rawlings, M., *Beyond Death's Door,* Sheldon Press, 1979, p 82.

29. Moody, R.A., *Life after Life,* Mockingbird *Books,* Covington, Georgia (Bantum edition), 1975, p 31.

30. Sabom, M.B., *Recollections of Death,* Corgi Edition, 1982, p 65.

31. Ibid. p 66.

32. Fenwick, P. and Fenwick, E. *The Truth in the Light,* BCA, 1995, p 76.

33. Sabom, M.B., *Recollections of Death,* Corgi Edition, 1982, p 68.

34. Atwater, P.M.H., *Beyond the Light,* (revised edition) Transpersonal, Kill Devil Hills, NC, 2009, p 47.

35. Sabom, M.B., *Recollections of Death,* Corgi Edition, 1982, p 69.

36. Barrett, W., *Death-Bed Visions,* Aquarian Press, Wellingborough, 1986, p 96-103.

37. Ibid. p 104.

38. Fenwick, P. and Fenwick, E. *The Truth in the Light,* BCA, 1995, p 89.

39. Sabom, M.B., *Recollections of Death,* Corgi Edition, 1982, p 69

40. Rawlings, M., *Beyond Death's Door,* Sheldon Press, 1979, p 98-99.

41. Brinkley, D., *Saved by the Light.* Piatkus Ltd, London, 1994, p26.

42. Rawlings, M., *Beyond Death's Door,* Sheldon Press, 1979, p 96-97

43. Fenwick, P. and Fenwick, E. *The Truth in the Light,* BCA, 1995, p 110-111.

44. Sabom, M.B., *Light and Death,* Zondervan, Michigan 1998, p 67.

45. Sabom, M.B., *Recollections of Death,* Corgi Edition, 1982, p 72.

46. Ring, K., *Life at Death. A scientific investigation of the Near-Death Experience,* Coward, Mc Cann and Geoghegan, 1981, p 63.

47. Rawlings, M., *Beyond Death's Door,* Sheldon Press, 1979, p 99.

48. Ibid. p 86-87.

49. Sabom, M.B., *Recollections of Death,* Corgi Edition, 1982, p 108

50. Atwater, P.M.H., *Beyond the Light,* (revised edition) Transpersonal, Kill Devil Hills, NC, 2009, p 53-54.

51. Fenwick, P. and Fenwick, E. *The Truth in the Light,* BCA, 1995, p 97.

52. Ibid. p 98.

53. Ibid. p 99.

54. Ibid. p 102.

55. Ibid. p 103.

56. Moody, R.A., *Life after Life,* Mockingbird *Books,* Covington, Georgia (Bantum edition), 1975, p 76.

57. Fenwick, P. and Fenwick, E. *The Truth in the Light,* BCA, 1995, p 104.

58. Ibid. p 109.

59. Moody, R.A., *Life after Life,* Mockingbird *Books,* Covington, Georgia (Bantum edition), 1975, p 80.

60. Ibid. p 65-66.

61. https://en.wikipedia.org/wiki/Life_review

62. Fenwick, P. and Fenwick, E. *The Truth in the Light,* BCA, 1995, p 114.

63. Eadie, B.J. *Embraced by the Light*, The Aquarian Press, HarperCollins, 1994.

64. Fenwick, P. and Fenwick, E. *The Truth in the Light,* BCA, 1995, p 115.

65.Grey, M. *Return from Death : An explanation of the Near-Death-Experience.* Arkana 1985, p 63.

66. Fenwick, P. and Fenwick, E. *The Truth in the Light,* BCA, 1995 p187-196.

67. Kubler-Ross, E. *On Children and Death.* Collier Books, 1983.

68. Morse, M., *et. al. Childhood Near-death-experiences.* American Journal of Diseases of Children. 1986, Vol. 140 .

69. Fenwick, P. and Fenwick, E. *The Truth in the Light,* BCA, 1995, p 172.

70. Sabom, M.B., *Light and Death,* Zondervan, Michigan 1998, p 37-51.

71. Ring, K and Cooper, S. *Mindsight : Near-Death and Out-of-Body Experiences in the Blind.* Morris Publishing, 1999.

72. Grof, S. *Books of the Dead : Manuals for Living and Dying,* Thomes and Hudson, 1994, p 31.

73. Fenwick, P. and Fenwick, E. *The Truth in the Light,* BCA, 1995, p 36.

74. Ibid. p130

75. Moody, R.A., *Life after Life,* Mockingbird *Books,* Covington, Georgia (Bantum edition), 1975, p 97.

76. Van Lommel, P. et.al. *Near-Death Experiences in survivors of cardiac arrest : a prospective study in the Netherlands.* Lancet, 2001 Vol. 358, p. 2039-2045

77. Kashner, S. and Schoenberger, N. *Furious Love : Elizabeth Taylor, Richard Burton and the Marriage of the Century.* JR Books, 2010

78. Warren, J. In Daily Express newspaper. Feb.11, 2013. p. 29.

79. http://www.allaboutheaven.org/observations/10498/221/peter-sellers-out-of-body-experience-012467.

80.http://www.zimbio.com/Celebrities+Who've+Brushed+with+Death/articles/wQ0rllaP1lY/Donald+Sutherland.

81. http://www.near-death.com/experiences/rich-and-famous.html (number 23).

82. http://www.friendsofjane.com/aaj_neardeath.html

83. http://www.near-death.com/experiences/rich-and-famous.html

(number 6).

84. Morse, M. *Parting Visions : An exploration of Pre-Death Psychic and Spiritual Experiences.* Platkus 1995.

85. Moody, R. and Perry, P. *Glimpses of Eternity : Sharing a loved one's passage from this life to the next.* New York. Guideposts, 2010.

86. http://edition.cnn.com/interactive/2014/12/us/shared-death/

87. Pasricha, S. and Stevenson, I. *Near-Death Experiences in India.* Journal of the American Society for Psychical Research 1986, 77, 1 15 - 135.

88. Otis, K. and Haraldsson, E. *At the Hour of Death.* 1977, New York, Avon Books.

89. Osis, K. and Haraldsson, E. *Deathbed observations by physicians and nurses : A cross-cultural survey.* Journal of the American Society for Psychical Research, 1977, 71, p. 237-259

90. Kreps, J. L. *The Search for Muslim Near-Death Experiences.* Journal of Near-Death Studies, 28 (2) 2009, p. 67-86.

91. Feng Zhi-ying and Liu Jian-xun. *Near-Death Experiences Among Survivors of the 1976 Tangshan Earthquake* . Journal of Near-Death Studies, 11 (1) 1992, p. 39-48.

92. Carter, C. *Science and the Near-Death Experience.* Inner Traditions, Rochester, Vermont. 2010, p 125.

93. Delog Dawa Drolma. *Journey to Realms beyond Death.* Pilgrims Publishing. New Edition 2002.

94. https://www.god-helmet.com/bkknde.htm

95. Murphy, T. *Near-Death experiences in Thailand.* Journal of Near-Death Studies, 2001, 19 (3).

96. Atwater, P.M.H., *Beyond the Light,* Carol Publishing Group, 1994, p. 242.

97. Ring, K., *Life at Death. A scientific investigation of the Near-Death Experience,* Coward, Mc Cann and Geoghegan, 1980.

98. Greyson, B. *The Near-Death Experience Scale: Construction, reliability, and validity*. Journal of Nervous & Mental Disease, 1983, *171,* 369-375.

99. Greyson, B. *Near-death encounters with and without NDEs.* Journal of Near-Death Studies 8 (3) 1990.

100. Morse M. *Parting Visions : A new scientific paradigm. The near-death-experience : a reader* In Bailey and Yates, eds. Routledge 1996 p.299-319.

101. Sabom, M.., *Recollections of Death,* Corgi Edition, 1982, Appendix.

102. Parnia, S. *et.al AWARE - AWAreness during REsuscitation - A prospective study.* Resuscitation, 2014, Vol. 85 (12), p. 1799-1805.

103. DeVries *et.al, Changes in cerebral oxygen uptake and cerebral electrical activity during defibrillation threshold testing.* Anesthesia Analgesia 1998, 87, p. 16-20.

104. Smith, D. S., W. Levy, M. Maris, and B. Chance. *Reperfusion hyperoxia in the brain after circulatory arrest in humans.* Anesthesiology, 1990, 73, p.12–19.

105. Van Lommel, P. *Near-death experience, consciousness, and the brain : a new concept about the continuity of our consciousness based on recent scientific research on near-death-experience in survivors of cardiac arrest.* World Futures, Routledge, 2006, 62, p. 134-151.

106. Strassman, R. and Oualls, R. *Dose-response study of N,N-dimethyltryptamine in humans : Neuroendocrine, autonomic and cardiovascular effects.*. Archives of General Psychiatry 1994, 51: 85–97.

107. Jansen, K., *Ketamine ; Dreams and Reality.* Multidisciplinary Association for Psychedelic Studies, 2001.

108. Blackmore S. *Dying to live: science and the near-death experience.* London: Grafton--an imprint of Harper Collins Publishers, 1993

109. Parnia, S. *What happens when we die.* Hay House. 2006, p. 19.

110. Medua, L. J., *Carbon dioxide therapy*, Springfield Illinois, 1950.

111. Noyes, R. and Kletti, R. *Depersonalization in response to life-threatening danger*. Comprehensive Psychiatry, 1977, 18, (4), p. 375-384.

112. Moody, R.A., *Life after Life,* Mockingbird *Books,* Covington, Georgia (Bantum edition), 1975, p 47-48.

113. Simeon, D and Knutelska, M. *An open trial of Nalthrexone in the treatment of depersonalization disorder*. Journal of Clinical Psychopharmacology, 25 (3) 2005, p 267-270.

114. www.nytimes.com/2008/03/27/health/nutrition/27best.html.

115. Honegger, B. *The OBE as a Near-Birth Experience*. In Roll, W. G., Beloff, J., and White, R. A. (Eds.). *Research in Parapsychology*. Scarecrow Press. 1983, p. 230-231.

116. Sagan, C. *Broca's Brain : Reflections on the Romance of Science.* New York, Random House, 1979.

117. Blackmore, S. *Near-Death Experiences: In or out of the body?*. Skeptical Inquirer, 1991, 16: 34-45.

118. French, C. *Near-Death Experiences in Cardiac Arrest Survivors*. Progress in Brain Research, 2005, 150: 351-367.

119. Lorimer, D. *Near-Death-Experience and The Nature of Consciousness.* Biomedical and Life Physics. Ed D.N. Ghista 1996 p 391-392.

120. Walach, H. and Hartmann, R. *Complementarity is a useful concept for consciousness studies. A Reminder.* Neuroendocrinology Letters, 2000, 21, p. 221-232.

121. Woerlee, G.M. *Review of Consciousness Beyond Life by Pim Van Lommel* , 2011 in *http://neardth.com/consciousness-beyond-life.php*

Printed in Great Britain
by Amazon

57135941R00081